AUTHOR &
GROW RICH

How To Write A Money-Making Book
In Only 12 Hours!

Morgan James Publishing • New York

AUTHOR & GROW RICH
How To Write A Money-Making Book In Only 12 Hours!

GLENN DIETZEL

Paperback ISBN: 978-1-60037-293-3

Hardcover ISBN: 978-1-60037-294-0

Published by:

MORGAN · JAMES
THE ENTREPRENEURIAL PUBLISHER™
www.morganjamespublishing.com

Morgan James Publishing, LLC
1225 Franklin Ave., Ste. 325
Garden City, NY 11530-1693
Toll Free 800-485-4943
www.MorganJamesPublishing.com

Habitat for Humanity®
Peninsula
Building Partner

Cover Design by:
Rachel Campbell
www.r2cdesign.com
rachel@r2cdesign.com

Interior Design by:
Kimberly Lydon Stevenson
SpotCOLOR Design
kim@spotcolordesign.com

ABOUT THE AUTHOR

G lenn Dietzel is the Founder of Awakened, LLC, a leading thought company in the Recommendation Age. He has been at the forefront of authoring and business coaching/consulting now for several years. Insuring his clients all over the world author their own book in record time, Glenn teaches them to simultaneously build a profitable business using the power of the Internet.

Glenn has been called a 'profit master' by his peers in the authoring and business world with his accelerated business authoring system where he teaches his clients to create $10,000, $20,000, $50,000 and higher programs and services. His work with joint venture partners has produced over 1.2 billion dollars of increased profits to their clients' bottom lines in the past six years.

As a former Vice Principal with two post-graduate degrees he set two Internet records replacing both his income and his wife's income in record time—127 days off an 22 page digital download—with a system he now teaches his clients. He went on to set another Internet record making his first $100,000 from this same 18 page digital download on a list of under 500 people in less than 3 months and with no joint venture partners.

From Hong Kong to Hawaii, Glenn teaches people how to appropriate the specific attitudes, skills and knowledge not taught in any MBA program using the power of Entrepreneurial Authoring and the Unconscious Credibility Marketing System™. The success of Glenn's authoring system provides a first in the authoring and publishing world: Instant access to a New York Publisher.

Glenn's Entrepreneurial Authoring program has been recognized throughout the entire industry, some of whom include:

- The marketing company to leading e-publishing giant, ADOBE

- Internet marketing experts Alex Mandossian, Stephen Pierce, Joel Comm, Jim Edwards and many others

- PR experts Rick Frishman and Dave Lakhani

- Beryl Wolk, Father of the T.V. Infomercial Proctor

- Imal Wagner (publicist to Mark Victor Hansen and Robert Allen),

- The leading T.V. show, 'Call For Help' with Leo Laporte

- Consultants to two U.S. Presidents

- Many mid-tier companies (under NDAs)

- Professionals from every organization including doctors, lawyers, dentists, chiropractors...

- Self-publishing guru, Dan Poynter

📖 Clients from more than 90 countries!

📖 And many, many others!

Glenn's revolutionary Entrepreneurial Authoring Mastermind Programs and his keynote addresses..._Entrepreneurial Authoring: How To Become A Millionaire Expert_ provide would-be authors with the personal attention to author their money-making book.

If you are ready to challenge your assumptions about the steps you must take to market yourself in the new millennium, you'll be glad that you met Glenn. Your personal and professional success has never been closer at hand with this book, **Author And Grow Rich: How To Write A Money-making Book In Only 12 Hours**...And Gain Instant Access To A New York Publisher!

DEDICATION

This book is the culmination of thousands of hours of hard work and the loyal support of many people who supported my dreams of helping others author and publish their legacy.

Paul Jackson, with whom I first shared the dream of building an online business by teaching authoring and publishing. Ronda Del Boccio, one of the brightest women I know, who spent countless hours going over this manuscript with me. Karen Leonard the woman who keeps me organized and rules with a soft touch. Fiona, my wife, without whose continual support and encouragement this book would have never been possible. And to all the people who have strengthened me in my walk with God and reiterated that life has purpose and meaning.

This book is also dedicated to all of my clients who have worked with me and my team to leave their own legacies. I have been privileged to work with some of the brightest minds today. Thanks for bringing me into your legacy.

And finally to all of you who read this book...if a former Vice Principal who personified to a 't' Robert Kiyosaki's poor dad in the series, Rich Dad Poor Dad, can do this, so can you! I look forward to helping you not only leave your legacy but live it today!

TESTIMONIALS

T he following are just some of the hundreds and hundreds of people who have been impacted in the system you will discover with **Author And Grow Rich!**

"Glenn Dietzel has finally done the impossible. He has made it simple for you to write a 100 page book in 12 hours, or more, not 47 months like it to me, and not hiring a professional writer. He makes sure you connect with a major publisher. He can make certain that not only will you get published, but you have a market to receive it! He understands the whole process. He is a powerful man with powerful insights that will allow you to get your powerful message out there. That is going to help you in your career. That is going to provide you a massive amount of revenue and introduce you to a much greater audience who now understands what you do. And what you do is really important! **Author And Grow Rich** will do this and so much more!"

JOEL BAUER. . . . . Author Of
How To Persuade People
Who Don't Want To Be Persuaded
http://www.infotainer.com

"After following the exercises laid out clearly in Glenn Dietzel's program, **Author And Grow Rich,** for my latest book, I realized this system is not unlike the system I use to help others lead super successful lives."

JOHN ASSARAF . . . . NY Times And Wall Street Journal
Best Selling Author
http://www. John Assaraf.com

"When it comes to authoring and publishing online no one knows more than Glenn Dietzel. He's knowledgeable, energetic, and fun...and I'm having him back again and again and again!"

LEO LAPORTE .... #1 'How-To' T.V. Show, *Call For Help TV*
http://www.CallForHelpTV.com

"After having shared the stage with Glenn Dietzel at the world's first BookCamp(tm), I personally witnessed how easy it is to author a best selling book with his system. Even though I have authored over 85 books myself, I discovered a fantastic new way to help me author even faster! You need his system in **Author And Grow Rich** to help you create the most powerful business card today-your book!"

DAN POYNTER .... New York Times Best Seller
http://www.ParaPublishing.com

"What Glenn teaches about rapid business development is not found in any MBA course. Wow, I am totally impressed!"

BALDASSARE MINAUDO.................. Venture Capitalist
Toronto, Canada

"I owe a debt of gratitude. The manuscript sat for 2 years as I put it on the back burner. If it weren't for the power of Glenn Dietzel's system in **Author And Grow Rich**, I would never have had the opportunity to get this book done. Glenn, you did a great job!"

DREW MILES .... Author Of
Zero To Success
http://www.ZeroToSuccess.com

"Glenn Dietzel takes away all the barriers to becoming an author and makes the writing process easy and simple. With his step by step methodology, anyone can write a book in a very short amount of time. This book is packed with exercises that will allow you to get past the fear of writing, stop procrastinating and write a book that has a built in audience who will be hungry for your information."

DEBBIE BERMONT. . . . . Author Of
Outrageous Business Growth
http://www.OutrageousBusinessGrowth.com

"The ability to express yourself with the written word is crucial today. Writing ezines, articles, books and web copy are a daily part of doing business, and any person who wants to succeed in business, especially online, needs to learn how to write. I've looked at a lot of programs and I've never seen a program as comprehensive as Glenn Dietzel's. His **Author And Grow Rich** book is a fantastic introduction to his holistic method of not only writing, publishing and promoting your book, but also for building an entire business around your book. Writing a book is the springboard from which you can build a speaking, consulting, coaching or entrepreneurial career. Glenn Dietzel teaches you how to write your book with your entire business plan in mind. He helps you develop a business plan which is comprehensive and adaptable. As an educator he is able to teach would be and current authors in a way other programs out there can't. I'd highly recommend

Glenn Dietzel's book and authoring programs to anyone who is serious about their business future."

MARNIE PEHRSON . . . . http://www.ideamarketers.com

"The great thing about what Glenn Dietzel writes about in his book, **Author And Grow Rich,** is that the whole system is designed to make your business work. When I first started Glenn Dietzel's system all I wanted to do was write a book. I never thought about the business that could be built around the book. The key is for you to do exactly what he tells you to do. It really works!"

SANDRA G BAILEY . . . . Author Of
Real Dogs Don't Eat Kibble!
http://www.TheNaturallyHealthyDog.com

"I believe that 90+% of people have a message inside them and that most people end up dying with that message inside of them. What Glenn Dietzel has done has enabled everyone to resurrect that message and convert that message to becoming an author through his system. All you have to do is plug into this by reading **Author And Grow Rich**. If you are ready for your life to be impacted, if you're ready for change, if you're ready for massive momentum and growth in your life, make the decision and move forward with this book. In fact, get everyone in your mastermind group to get this book-better yet, purchase one for everyone-and leverage the power contained on the pages in **Author And Grow Rich**."

ED ZIMBARDI . . . . http://www.FulfillmentCentral.com

"Glenn Dietzel is the man who can take you through the process of authoring and publishing so painlessly you won't even believe it is possible. His process will take you through the creation of your book without pain and suffering and staying awake at night. I recommend his system to anyone who is ready to witness the power of his system in **Author And Grow Rich**."

DR. JILL AMMON-WEXLER . . . . Author And
Pioneer Brain/Mind Researcher
http://www.drjill.biz

"Glenn Dietzel's material has changed my life. **Author And Grow Rich** tells you how to write your book very, very simply. Glenn Dietzel has a number of unique methods, including his genealogy tree system that breaks things down into very simple components that allows you to write easily and effortlessly. People who want to write a book often say they have no time, but his methods show you how to author a book in 12 hours. Lastly, Glenn Dietzel always delivers on his promises. I am very, very impressed and happy!"

DR. LARRY SMITH. . . . . Author Of
Embracing The Journey Of Recovery
http://www.EmbracingTheJourneyBook.com

"If you want to truly succeed and be an **Author And Grow Rich** there is no one better qualified than Glenn Dietzel. In fact, there's one concept alone in the first chapter that once you grasp it, it will explode your success as an author and even your life. It's that powerful. The great thing about this book is that not only does it teach you step by step where to go, what to do, and how to do it, but it brings everything together. It takes you as the writer and your target market and ties them together and something amazing happens. First, you get to be recognized as an authority and you get to make an impact about what you're talking and writing about. Glenn Dietzel lays it out for you step by step. You need to get this book, read it and more importantly, you need to act on it. Do exactly what he says and you will get published-and you will be rich!"

ANDY DUNCAN . . . . http://www.netslingers.com

"I rarely give testimonials. However, Glenn Dietzel surpasses my expectations with everything he does. Glenn Dietzel is one of the top experts-hands-down-in this world in the field of authoring and publishing. He is of the highest ethical caliber and this is reflected in the quality of his book, **Author And Grow Rich**."

LEN FOLEY. . . . . Author Of
Sales Without The Sucker Punch
http://www.lenfoley.com

"To become an expert and authority in whatever your niche, you need to let the rest of the world know. Glenn Dietzel has created a new resource that will allow you to get vision and direction. **Author And Grow Rich** will take the knowledge inside your brain, take your concepts and ideas to a new audience and propel you to the expert level that you desire to be so that you can get the revenue you want in order to do whatever it is that you wish to do. Not only will Glenn Dietzel help you, but he will put you in touch with a New York Publisher.

Make a mess of this book and put it into action. Read this cover to cover."

Joel Comm . . . . New York Times Best-Selling Author, *The Adsense Code* http://www.joelcomm.com

"It used to be that an author would go through the traditional routes and starve. With Glenn Dietzel's new book, **Author And Grow Rich,** you will witness why Glenn Dietzel is fast becoming one of the most sought after speakers for his cutting edge ability to create processes to revolutionize industries with his coaching clients. In **Author And Grow Rich,** he will coach you the through the authoring process. Nothing provides you more credibility than to say, "Can I give you a copy of my book?" With Glenn's book, you will feel the amazing feeling of saying, "I am an author!"

Mike Stewart . . . . http://www.TeleseminarTools.com

"There are so many reasons why you must write your book, but the credibility you gain is huge-your "C" factor goes up 1000%! I wish I had read this before. One of the most difficult factors is writer's block. Glenn Dietzel shows you many ways to avoid this problem in his new resource. I am writing another book using his system. There is one secret alone that will double my sales which involves the most important factor to hook your reader. Glenn Dietzel is the real deal. His teaching is contagious as you will witness. I wholeheartedly endorse this new book."

Frank Sousa . . . . http://www.TrafficGeyser.com

"**Author And Grow Rich** will help you focus your passion with a market place. I have personally witnessed this power, and now I'm hearing back from people all over the world about what a difference my book is making. With Glenn Dietzel's New York Publisher, I now have the credibility to reach an international audience! Get **Author And Grow Rich** and discover the power that has launched both my business and my 501 (c) 3 to international fame!"

MARGARET MERRILL. . . . . Author Of
Live The Life You Love
http://www.FulfillYourPurpose.com

"How do you take that book in your mind and turn it into a book that is in book stores? Glenn Dietzel has a system that will help you turn it into a book in less than 12 hours! Think you have no time? Glenn Dietzel taught me in less than 12 hours. Get your hands on **Author And Grow Rich** immediately and get ready to change your life!"

FRANK GASIOROWSKI . . . . Author Of
90 Day Goals
http://www.90daysgoals.com

"I have an important story to share with people, but I've had a very socially unacceptable lifestyle in so many ways. I was afraid people wouldn't be receptive to a person like me sharing good news with them. Glenn Dietzel's system in **Author And Grow Rich** convinced me that people out there would want to hear from someone like me, especially since I did a 180 degree change in my life. And he was right! So, I can't put a high enough value on working with Glenn Dietzel and the system he has created in his new book. Glenn has delivered on everything that he has promised and more!"

KEN JENSEN . . . . Author Of
It Takes Guts To Be Me!
http://www.ItTakesGutsToBeMe.com

"As an ex-airline pilot I can now say the sky is the limit after working thru Glenn Dietzel's process laid out in **Author And Grow Rich**. I call getting your system an everyday miracle! Thank you, Glenn!"

BERT BOTTA . . . . Author Of
Blown Across The Sky On Great Winds
http://www.AviatorsJourneyToGod.com

"I have admired Glenn Dietzel from the beginning not only for the instant success he generated for himself, but most importantly for the work that he does with aspiring authors and those who can't seem to make any money with their writing. In his new book, **Author And Grow Rich**, Glenn Dietzel presents one of the most cutting edge systems I have witnessed. I know personally why so many leading professionals want to work with you!"

MICHAEL ANGIER . . . . Author Of
World Class Business Systems
http://www.successnet.org

"First off I want to tell you that Glenn Dietzel is a true champion. If you have not made the decision yet to have Glenn Dietzel and his system in **Author And Grow Rich** mentor you, you must make this decision today. I love what he's doing to change people's lives. Glenn, you're amazing!"

JOHN DI LEMME . . . . Author Of
Find Your Why
http://www.FindYourWhy.com

"I wish I'd known about Glenn Dietzel and his new book, **Author And Grow Rich**, 10 years ago when I wrote my own book. I self published and spent a ton of money in the process. It took me over a year to write this-an entire year of my life! It was after seeing the hundreds of books in my basement that I realized that I was responsible for selling my books. Glenn Dietzel's new service is so valuable to any would be author. I would have saved so much money and so much time had I had access to **Author And Grow Rich**. I highly recommend Glenn's system to you. Get this book!

DR. SCOTT LEWIS . . . . Performer At The Riviera
http://www.VegasHypnotist.com

"The process that Glenn Dietzel shares with you in **Author And Grow Rich** is what I used to author, The Executive Speaks. Glenn Dietzel also showed me that anything is possible if you really want it. Glenn Dietzel's process will teach you what it has done for me such has how to build a profitable business. In my case, I was formerly the CEO of the largest bank in

Trinidad and now I mentor C-Level Executives in the area of professional speaking."

PHILIP ROCHFORD . . . . Author Of
The Executive Speaks
http://www.nurturinglife.com

"In my first month on the Internet starting with nothing, I've made $1,000 in profit and created an e-mail list with 600 subscribers. More importantly, I now have access to all the experts in my field and they view me as an equal expert as well. Glenn Dietzel's material in **Author And Grow Rich** will open up a new paradigm for you about what is possible. Thank you so much, Glenn!"

MIKE SNYDER. . . . . http://www.TheRawDiet.com

"After listening to Glenn Dietzel and following his system set forth so clearly in **Author And Grow Rich**, I really learned how to market to people's wants. Glenn Dietzel's system is an easy to follow, step by step, fill-in-the-dots system that works. After all he is an educator. In fact, I just launched my eBook and sold 123 copies and earned $2,948.31 in one evening following what he teaches. Following Glenn Dietzel's advice about joint ventures, I made just over $3,000 USD in my first week! Glenn, thanks for doing what you do so well!"

MARJAN GLAVAC . . . . Author Of
How To Make A Difference
http://www.TheBusyEducator.com

"I had the experience of trying to write my own eBook. I spent about 3 weeks trying to do it, and in the end of those 3 weeks I had about 6 pages done and a lot of frustration and hassle. Going through Glenn Dietzel's program in **Author And Grow Rich**, and learning how to do it appropriately using his system, in those same 3 weeks I had a 75 page eBook completed and a lot less head ache and hassle. I was much more focused and I can't say enough about this system. Thank you, Glenn!"

MIKE CORDON . . . . Author Of
Make Your Body Lean
http://www.MakeYourBodyLean.com

"From ebooks to marketing to building a business, Glenn Dietzel is hands down the very best! I would highly recommend his system to anyone who is ready to write a book, or take their career and business to the next level. With Glenn Dietzel's materials I have been able to take my coaching business to a new level. Because of his system, I've gone from no business and 0 clients to over 50 clients worldwide in only four months. I am now known as one of the top success coaches in the world. And I've just published with his New York Publisher! Get your hands on **Author And Grow Rich** quick and become the noted expert in your field! It works!"

SCOTT ARMSTRONG. . . . . Author Of
Boston Marathon Or Bust
http://www.bouldercoachingacademy.com

"In this highly complicated world it is always refreshing to find an industry expert who can take what seems to be an arduous task like writing a book and simplify it to become more of a common sense, no-nonsense project. That's exactly what Glenn Dietzel has done with his amazing system for turning your passion into a profitable book and business. I cannot give a recommendation any stronger than the one I am giving Glenn Dietzel. Thank you Glenn for what you do so well!"

TOM BEAL . . . . http://www.TheSalesChampion.com

"Glenn Dietzel not only is an expert in teaching the success formula for writing, he's also incredibly astute with bringing the best out of you. When you start to think you're ready to build your cash flow get Glenn Dietzel's new book, **Author And Grow Rich**. He'll take you to where you can truly flourish like he has done for me!"

FAWN CHRISTIANSON. Los Angeles, CA

"Glenn Dietzel gave me a roadmap for developing an e-book. His system helped shave considerable time from the process and has helped me to avoid a lot of mistakes. His **Author And Grow Rich** system is a definite must if you are even considering writing a book."

NAJEEB SIDDIQUE . . . . Atlanta, Georgia

"If you have ever entertained a thought about writing a book then Glenn's system is for you. You will learn what you need to know to get it done-and get it done quickly. Wow!"

DON STEELE. . . . . San Antonio, Texas

"Get your hands on all of Glenn Dietzel's programs. His success with clients globally is the ultimate proof that what he teaches in his new resource, **Author And Grow Rich**, will do that for you as well!"

EVA ALMEIDA . . . . Publisher
http://www.eBooksnBytes.com

"Your authoring system for helping entrepreneurs create expert status is terrific! It's really good! It's easy to read and well laid out. There is nothing currently available that teaches the authoring process from a teaching perspective. And if that in and of itself is not enough reason for you to get his new book **Author And Grow Rich**, then realize that what Glenn Dietzel really shares is how to build a profitable business using the power of the Internet. This is truly the definitive resource today to **Author And Grow Rich!**"

DEBRA KIMBROUGH. . . . . Author Of Numerous Books
http://www.debrakimbrough.com

If you want to unleash your greatness and build an information business online you need a book. Look no further than Glenn Dietzel. I have witnessed personally how his system has created a successful business. Glenn Dietzel shows people, even with no writing experience, how to author a successful eBook. It's unbelievable! Imagine writing a book facing no writer's block. Just think, you can join the ranks of those making an additional source of income from the Internet very easily with a system that works. Take focused action now. Who knows, I might be interviewing you in my next best seller!"

MIKE LITMAN . . . . Best Selling Author Of
Conversations with Millionaires
http://www.MikeLitman.com

"Most books stop at what you 'need to know' but you take it much farther with your clear and defined start to finish process. The brainstorming process coupled with the system on analyzing your business potential forced me to focus my actions and made the creating of content simple and painless knowing all along my business potential. I am definitely a Believer now. Glenn Dietzel's, **Author And Grow Rich**, will go on my desk as a reference manual for all my writing and business projects. Great Job!"

JOE GARRIS . . . . Cincinnati Ohio
www.ProductIdeaEvaluator.com

"What was the elusive ingredient that was missing in this writer's dream of getting published? FOCUS! Glenn Dietzel absolutely got me on the right track to taking my obscure, partially finished manuscript, sitting dusty and forlorn on my computer's hard drive, and taking it to book heaven! His system in **Author And Grow Rich** has definitely Awakened The Author in me. Thanks Glenn!!

DARREL R. WALROD........................... Author Of
7 Little Known, Ultra-Classified Secrets
Your Banker Will Never Tell You
http://www.CreditYourAccount.com

"I was already a published author, but without the entrepreneurial foundation. Because of Glenn Dietzel and his system found in **Author And Grow Rich,** I have a clear vision of how to turn a book into a business."

KALINDA ROSE STEVENSON..................... Author Of
No Money Limits
http://www.NoMoneyLimits.com

"If you even suspect you've got a book or ebook inside of you Glenn Dietzel will definitely show you how to make that become a reality and then control your market."

SHAUN FAWCETT.............. Author Of Numerous Books
http://www.Writinghelptools.com

"Glenn has truly transformed my thinking and daily actions necessary to be successful! Glenn's expertise in the areas of authoring, publishing and personal empowerment have completely transformed me into possessing the right knowledge, skills and attitudes to become a successful author and business owner.

For example, my previous e-book took me 300+ hours to write and edit. With Glenn's direction my next book was easily finished in less than 12 hours. Within the next month I will make my first $100,000 on the Internet with a specific action plan to make my first $1 million by year's end! Thank you, Glenn!"

SHAWN WIEDERIN . . . . Author Of
What Mom And Dad Should Have
Taught Me About Money
Cedar Springs, Iowa

"I've already experienced a revenue increase of over $15,000 in less than 60 days thanks to Glenn Dietzel's system of authoring focused on business profit! Get **Author And Grow Rich** immediately and apply his concepts to your passion."

LORRAINE LANE . . . . Business Consultant
Tampa, Florida

"Since applying Glenn Dietzel's system in **Author And Grow Rich**, our new patients are up 75% in a matter of six weeks and our new services up 15% in this same time frame."

DR. KEVIN KAURICH . . . . South Bend, Indiana

"Before I started working with the process that Glenn teaches in **Author And Grow Rich**, my entire business was just a pipe dream. I felt overwhelmed with tons of ebooks, cd's, seminar notes, teleseminar notes, etc. I also felt frustrated and disappointed with the amount of time that I had put into trying to create my business and yet had generated no income. I have worked with many of the 'big names' that we have all heard of in the internet industry. Each of them provided me with lots of helpful information, but no way to put it all together. Working with Glenn Dietzel's system changed all of that.

BRIDGET COPLEY . . . . San Francisco, CA

"My business has generated more clients and revenue in the tail end of the year than it did the whole year long! Again, "solid results" is the best thing to say about what Glenn Dietzel teaches in **Author And Grow Rich**. He is a great, mentor!"

DOREEN BANASZAK . . . . http://www.GetUnslumped.com

"Working with Glenn Dietzel has been an amazing experience, both for me personally and for my business. What he can bring to the students I am working with, just enriches where they are going with their projects who want to give back in life. I was able to learn to let go of fear and never give up, and now I have been able to work with Glenn Dietzel to bring that to the public in my book. I have been able to use my personal experiences, and the opportunity it has given me to reach out to others and give them hope. Glenn, I thank you for what you bring to me personally and to my family in letting me share my story. Get his new book, **Author And Grow Rich**, and prove it for yourself!"

SHERRY WATSON . . . . Author And
Leading Grant Writing Expert
http://www.ThePowerOfGrantMoney.com

"The system that Glenn Dietzel teaches in **Author And Grow Rich** did more for us in 6 weeks than the previous year and a half. I was able to quit my Systems Engineering job within 9 months! The importance of your book gives you personal and professional credibility. Our book brings us a steady stream of clients 24/7. Chapter 8 showed me what was missing in my book and enabled us to publish books that we didn't even know existed. You need to get this book now."

WES WADDELL . . . . Author Of
Scrap Booking In The Digital Age
http://www.princesscrafts.com

"For the last 16 years I have always wanted to write my book. I used the principles found in **Author And Grow Rich** and, two months later, it is finished and I have been accepted by Glenn Dietzel's New York Publisher. What an incredible system! Thank you Glenn!"

ANNA OLSON . . . . Author Of
Growing Up Amish
http://www.growingupamish.com

"Your book makes you an authority to up sell products and services as an expert to get speaking engagements so that you can build your business easily. Don't be afraid. It's not a hard process when you work with experts. Glenn Dietzel and his system in **Author And Grow Rich** will help you to be on TV, magazines...make the money you know you deserve! Thank you, Glenn. You have helped make my clients famous!"

IMAL WAGNER . . . . Publicist For
World Class Authors And Speakers
http://www.imalwagner.com

FOREWORD

Author And Grow Rich As An Entrepreneurial Author

I am an Entrepreneurial Author and so are all of the authors with Morgan James Publishing. You too can become an Entrepreneurial Author!

Being an Entrepreneurial Author is about having the right mindset and approach to your book, just like Glenn Dietzel presents here in **Author And Grow Rich**. It's also about learning how to profit from your book, and making the most out of your opportunities.

What Does It Mean To Be An Entrepreneurial Author?

Entrepreneurial Authors are concerned first and foremost for the readers of their book. They think about the benefits that the readers will gain by buying and reading the book. They also think in terms of the customers, the clients, or the constituency they serve.

Entrepreneurial Authors know that they will make the most money from what their book does for them—not from the royalties of that book. They see their book royalties as a small bonus for writing a book, but not the reason for writing a book.

Entrepreneurial Authors see their book as a way to become a celebrity in their market—as a way to gain instant expert status.

Entrepreneurial Authors understand that a book is a powerful lead generation tool that can help grow their customer and prospect databases—customers, or prospects who may go on to become life-long customers. They see their book as one of the tools for the top of their marketing funnel.

Entrepreneurial Authors understand that a book can give them access to markets that they otherwise would not have had access to. They know that a book can open up new markets for them, providing access to new customers, new clients and new partners.

Entrepreneurial Authors understand that they can gain new speaking engagements and other opportunities to get in front of their target audience. "Now introducing Glenn Dietzel, author of the bestselling book, *Author and Grow Rich*," is a familiar sounding announcement when Glenn goes on stage. Having a book title follow your name is a powerful credibility tool.

Entrepreneurial Authors take advantage of all of the publicity and recognition that their book gives them in their local market and beyond. They also use their book, or the fact that they have been accepted by a publisher, to gain all of the publicity and recognition they can.

Entrepreneurial Authors use their book to help them develop additional products. Examples could be a reading of the same book to create an audio CD product, a home-study course based on the principles of the book, or a work book to compliment the content of the book.

Entrepreneurial Authors are prepared to build a very large business from the success of their book, the additional clientele their book brings, and the celebrity status their book gives. If they have an existing business, the book is a tool or an additional product or lead generator to augment their current success.

Entrepreneurial Authors are prepared to write their book in a manner that provides benefits to both their readers and to themselves. Their book is a tool for earning profit and entrepreneurial authors recognize this and enjoy the benefits of the profit their book brings. For some entrepreneurial authors, publishing a book will make them more money with their current 9 to 5 job, by way of possible promotions, outside opportunities or newfound credibility.

The Marketing Funnel

Understanding the marketing funnel is one of the most basic, yet most important, lessons in marketing. The entire premise of the marketing funnel is the idea of the 80/20 rule, also known as Pareto's law. The 80/20 rule simply states that

80% of your results will be generated by only 20% of your activities. Said another way: 80% of your revenue/income will come from 20% of your clients.

Now imagine there is a funnel, or inverted triangle. At the top of the funnel you have many customers or prospects that have bought a small-ticket product from you, or perhaps have merely requested information about your company or products.

At the bottom of the funnel you would find fewer customers or clients, but those who resulted in a greater percentage of profits for your business.

In order to find those "whale" customers, you must start by finding many "minnow" customers. As some of your customers get to know you better, like what you do, and trust you, they're likely to purchase more from you and will naturally graduate down the funnel and become higher paying clients. Those who continue through your marketing funnel can also be developed into lifelong customers. Lifelong, evangelistic customers are a business' greatest source of revenue and profits.

Your job is to find out what your customers (or target market) want, and deliver it to them. Glenn will talk more about this later. He will also tell you how you can have your target market decide on your book content for you.

Danielle Steel learned how to do this and became a huge success. She knew how to deliver what women wanted to read, though she didn't know a comma from a colon. In Women's Day, June, 1990, Steel said, "I am never lonely when I write. You concoct dream men because there are no men in your life."

Action Exercise:

Think about just one additional product or service that you could offer your clientele that you're not currently offering. It could be a big ticket item (over $1,000) or a small ticket item (under $1,000). Simply think of a new product or service that you're not yet offering and write it down.

Here is a perfect example...

100 people buy a copy of your book

25 go online to claim the free bonus that you offer in your book

10 purchase a $97 audio recording from you

3 purchase a $397 home-study course

1 person hires you for consulting at $1,000/hour or attends your $5,000 seminar

But, It's Not Just About Dollars And Cents

Entrepreneurial Authors do more than read books and attend seminars about achievement to success. They take action, do something, and shake the tree.

They know that their time on Earth is limited, that the most important time is right now, and they've got to get it right the first time. To do this, they go with the flow—their own flow—possessing the sensitivity to know what they really want, what they can do well, why they're here, what they love to do, what is realistic, and what is possible.

Entrepreneurial Authors Understand Their Clients

An entrepreneurial author is by definition a good marketer. A good marketer understands his or her client base—as well as the target market.

Considering all aspects of your ideal customer or target client may not be necessary at this time. However, it's a good idea for you to get a feel for whom you will be writing your book.

The more closely you can understand and associate with your ideal customer from your target market, the more impact your book, or any other material you create, will have. I believe in providing value to the greatest number of people possible.

That's where the idea for our publishing model came

from. We desired to serve more authors and more business people than traditional publishers did. Most people know that even getting an audience with a traditional publisher can be a trying experience—let alone if you get picked up. Our goal was different.

Our goal has always been to see publishing from the point of view of our clients—those people whose businesses, lives, and careers would be positively impacted by writing and having a published book.

In this same way, put yourself in the shoes of those you wish to serve. What's going on in their minds? What are their fears and concerns? What are they hopeful about? What do they look forward to?

When you answer these questions, you'll begin to develop a clearer vision for what your book will be about and what your content should include.

Action Exercise:

Write down the answers to the following questions:

- 📖 Who would you like to write your book for? i.e. Who do you think should be reading it, or would benefit from reading your book?

- 📖 What information, knowledge, skills, or experiences would you like to share with this group of people you desire to serve?

📖 After putting yourself in this person's shoes, what comes to mind? What are the concerns and aspirations they have?

📖 What are some of the ways that you can help alleviate their fears and concerns?

📖 What are some of the ways that you can help inspire or advance their goals and dreams?

Now, What Are The Bottom-Line Advantages Of Becoming An Entrepreneurial Author?

📖 You will earn more money in your present job or career

📖 You will become the acclaimed expert in your field

📖 You will gain celebrity status

📖 You will become the go-to expert in your market

📖 You will have access to new speaking platforms

📖 You will reach customers that you never reached before

📖 You will expand your sphere of influence

Casual Observation

Consider some of the most successful people that you know. What do many of them have in common? Many very successful people in society today either became famous and successful, in part, because of the book(s) they had written, or otherwise had written about their success after-the-fact.

If you consider a guest on a daytime news or talk show, what often will appear after their name?

"Today as our guest we have Mr. John Smith, author of the book _____."

Isn't that how many guests are introduced? For those who are sharp enough to recognize the opportunities inherent in writing a book and having it published, there is a world of potential.

When I wrote my first book, I became the go-to expert in my local community as a mortgage banker. Why? Simply because I was the only person who had written a book and had it published.

There is a mysterious phenomenon that happens when you become the author of a published book. For some reason that still escapes me, you become the expert. Having a book published gives its author tremendous credibility.

I learned this lesson from one of my coaches, Jay Conrad Levinson. Jay is best known as the father of Guerrilla Marketing and is a best-selling author with more than 14 million books sold. One of the principles of Guerrilla Marketing is to do everything you can to establish yourself as an expert.

The expert is the person that people go to for solutions and advice. The expert is the person they often trust first. When you write your book and get it published, you'll have taken a critical step in becoming an expert.

You will have a lead generation tool that will help you make more sales in your business. Your book will help you create other products and services to sell to your growing customer database. If you don't have a customer list, then your book will help you create one. Your book will justify your method of doing whatever it is you do. Your clients will entrust you with their business because they'll see you as "the one that wrote the book on it." Your business will expand.

Most people truly have a book in them. What book is in you?

I personally believe that most people have several books in them. Raise your hand if there is one topic about which you could talk for hours and hours. What's the topic? Is it stamps, cars, sailing, golf, your career, an admired author or actor? What topic draws you into a conversation?

Even the quietest people you know have something they love to talk about. Think for a minute about those people in your life. Now think about the person who is the quiet one. When speaking with that person, if a topic is brought up in the conversation that they enjoy, how lively and animated does his or her conversation become? What topic brings out your animated side?

You probably never thought of your passion as something that could turn into a book. Believe me, it can! I've seen books that are written on ordinary, everyday topics become best sellers. For instance, Suze Orman is one of the leading experts on money and investing. Her latest book, Women & Money, is targeted specifically to teaching women how to take control of their financial future. Guess what? It was an instant New York Times best-seller. Why? Aren't there plenty of books on the market that teach finances to the masses? Sure! But in this book, Suze took something as simple as finances and targeted the female gender, and in doing so created an overnight success.

What do you do that is targeted for a specific market? Do you know what your target market would be? If you haven't already done so, take a few minutes and complete the Action Exercise above. Think about what you are passionate about and write it down. Make bullets on the things you know about your subject. Those bullets could bring about enough content for several books—or at least a start for several books.

You might be pleasantly surprised about what you know that you hadn't really thought of before now. Remember, just because you know a lot about a topic, doesn't mean that everyone else has the same knowledge.

Share what you know... and you can **Author And Grow Rich!**

DAVID L. HANCOCK
Author of **The Entrepreneurial Author** and
Founder of Morgan James Publishing

TABLE OF CONTENTS

PREFACE

My Story As A Former Vice Principal

Not that long ago I was a Vice Principal. I had become our board's youngest Vice Principal and was ready to fast track it to what I believed was freedom...working my way up the "corporate" ladder to becoming a superintendent and eventually a Director of Education.

That sounded impressive to my parents. It impressed my friends. Even my wife was excited about this! However, there was only one person hesitant about my direction. Me.

For a number of years I had been realizing that although I loved to work with children, being a teacher was just not doing it for me. I also could not see myself doing anything else in life. Why? Because I had no confidence in my abilities. I surely didn't know what I know now, but inside of me I became acutely aware that I had a story running in the back of my head about why I didn't deserve success.

And boy was it powerful!

It played constant messages about stories and situations that had occurred in my past. The problem with these stories is that they were so powerful that they literally held me back from getting out of my comfort zone. The sad thing that I realized later on was that my comfort zone—indeed everyone's comfort zone—is a metaphor for the box that each of us has created for our existence.

And comfort zones are so constraining. The box that you confine yourself to live in is established out of the fears that you internalize beginning in the earliest years of your existence.

My fears were a combination of being a victim of sexual abuse as a young boy where nothing was done about it, and living in a household where emotional health was not taught.

The Day Of Reckoning

Everybody needs a wakeup call. Everybody needs to realize they have a big dream. You need to realize that you have a big dream. You need to realize that there is purpose in life and that never has it been easier to fulfill your purpose and leave a legacy while you make a difference in the lives of people globally.

Your day of reckoning comes when you realize that life really begins when you gain emotional independence.

Let me take a moment for an Aside...Because I firmly believe that unless you gain emotional independence over your own life, you will never realize your big dream in life, we have created for you a FREE 2CD Set (Value $154 USD) to help you gain your own emotional independence so that you can move forward in life with legacy building confidence.

"The Journey To The Person You Must Become:
Use The Revolutionary FA²ST™ System
And The Latest In Brain
And Optimum Performance Research
To Awaken Your Personal Legacy"

Go now and get this FREE CD Set (Value $154 USD)
http://ThePersonYouMustBecome.com

My day of reckoning was when I began an intensive counseling program to begin to establish my own emotional independence. This set me free to begin building an Internet based business to help those with a desire to author a book and build an information empire around their area of passion.

Not long afterward, I received a phone call from ADOBE...the world's leader in e-publishing. At that time I was working hard to get out of my job as a Vice-Principal with a website that focused on helping educators author, publish and market their expertise. The woman I spoke to who represented ADOBE could not believe that an educator was leading the world in the area of authoring and publishing.

He Set Two Internet Records!

A year later I launched AwakenTheAuthorWithin.com, and within 127 days, I replaced my income as a Vice Principal and my wife's income as an Occupational Therapist without any joint venture partners and beginning from scratch—faster than anyone I know and thanks to the Internet. Two months later I fulfilled my contract with my Board of Education and left my job for good!

Within three months of going full time, I made my first $100G on the Internet with a list of fewer than 500 people and an incomplete manuscript launched as a 22-page digital book...again another Internet record.

Today, I fly the world over. Our Entrepreneurial Authoring program is recognized as the only training authoring program that facilitates from a teaching perspective the attitudes, skills and knowledge necessary to distinguish one's book and build an Internet business at the same time.

Author And Grow Rich is a synthesis of this program with the aim to transform the business model and paradigm of the poor author into the realm of riches. The purpose of **Author And Grow Rich** is to show you that you don't have to be a J.K. Rowling or a Stephen King to make money. In fact, thanks to the Internet and e-publishing, you can build a thriving business from your own home. All you need is a laptop and a wireless connection and you can literally begin to live your legacy within a matter of hours.

This book will provide you the basics to write your book faster than you ever dreamed possible. The purpose of this book is to also to get you started on a sure footing in order to build a successful business using the power of the Internet. It is hoped that you will invest in the Entrepreneurial Authoring Home Study Program or in the Entrepreneurial Authoring Executive Mastermind Program which will provide you the deeper nuggets to move you along.

Guaranteed Instant Access To A New York Publisher

For example, in the Entrepreneurial Authoring Home Study Program we provide you with access to three live teleseminars, 8 taped teleseminars on how to use the Entrepreneurial Authoring Manual and several dozen taped calls where we work with others just like you. In this way we are able to help you personalize the material for your own specific wants. This program also provides you the powerful guarantee that you will gain instant access to a New York Publisher!

Guaranteed Instant Access With A New York Publisher

Many who own the **Author And Grow Rich** book decide to invest in this program and many decide to invest in the Entrepreneurial Authoring Executive Mastermind Program. With this program you not only receive instant access to a New York Publisher, we assure you that your book will get accepted or we will complete the book for you! This program hand- holds you thru the entire process for 6 months...a first in the industry of authoring and publishing.

The Power of the **Author And Grow Rich** program is that it shows you exactly how to author a 100-page book in less than 12 hours of actual writing time. **Author and Grow Rich** shows you not only how to write a book faster than you every dreamed possible, but never face writer's block again. Never!

This book also teaches you how to think like a savvy business person using fundamental principles of sales and marketing not taught in any MBA program anywhere!

Author And Grow Rich shows budding writers how to understand and put into action their uniqueness in the market place to ensure that your book stands out in the crowd by creating your own USP—universal sales/selling proposition.

Author and Grow Rich teaches you how to access your own million-dollar story, which we call your UPP (Your Unique

Personal Proposition). Yes, you have a million dollar story and we will show you how to access it and incorporate it into your book so that you are ready to be featured in the media.

Author and Grow Rich shows you how to know, even before putting pen to paper, that your book will sell—big time.

Author and Grow Rich teaches you how to take your Table Of Contents (TOC) and write winning "copy" (the words that you use to attract others to make an investment in your book and other products and services that you provide) and compel readers to buy your book because YOU can help them solve their problems.

- Nothing beats the satisfaction of confidently structuring your thoughts on paper with a winning, personalized formula...that works EVERY TIME!

- Nothing beats the self-assurance that you will NEVER again be "condemned to the pit of mental hell" with the dreaded disease "writer's block." With this system, your thoughts will rush out of you faster than you imagined possible.

Get ready to leave your comfort zone in the dust and propel yourself into action. It's time to make your big dream a reality!

Joel Comm came to me for business mentoring. His book, *The AdSense Code* hit #5 on the New York Times Best Seller list for business books in July of 2006 using our New York Publisher. Joel continues to grow his business around the needs of his hungry market. Joel has gone on to build a multi-million dollar online empire and is one of the biggest names in the Internet speaking world.

Visit Joel at http://www.TheAdsenseCode.com.

INTRODUCTION

This book and my Entrepreneurial Authoring program developed because I had to get myself on a different path. I was deeply mired in debt, and I needed to get myself on the path to wealth. Not only did I do that for my family and me, but I created this book and a successful business because my wife helped me find focus.

You Want To Write A Book—I Know You Do

I know you have a dream of writing a book. How do I know? Well, for one thing, you're reading this book right now. But I have statistical proof as well. According to the Association Of American Publishers, 83% of the American public confesses to having a book in them that they want to write. That's huge. And I will show you how to leverage that book you have inside you for all it's worth to make you a wealthy problem solver.

Your Ticket To Freedom

Do you want to experience a life that is open to possibilities for you? Do you want to experience the power of making a difference in the world? Do you want to experience the absolute power and joy of attracting a loyal following of people who want what you know and are willing to pay you money for the attitudes, skills and knowledge that you possess?

Don't sell yourself short. Your passion, your talents, your life experiences can make you money! That's right! People all over the world are willing to spend money on what you know and what you have figured out thru the school of hard knocks.

Who Should Read This Book

If you are a successful business person

If you are an entrepreneur

If you are a stay at home mom

If you are a woman working outside of the home

If you are in debt

If you are gravely in debt

If you are successful

If you are really successful

If you are disillusioned with the educational system

If you got an A in English

If you flunked high school English

In short—YOU! You should read this book.

Why? As stated above, 83% of Americans want to write a book, and you probably have this dream. In fact you must have this dream, or you wouldn't have bought this book, right?

It does not matter your IQ score. It does not matter how successful you have been in your ability to write in the past. It does not matter what others have told you about why you can't write.

What does matter is the story that you have been telling yourself about why you don't deserve success. In fact, the first thing you must do before you proceed with reading this book is to order the FREE CD set (value $154) from **The Person You Must Become.** Go now to get this website at http://ThePersonYouMustBecome.com.

You will discover how to develop legacy building confidence to accomplish your big dream.

Your Book Is Your Ticket To Freedom

In fact, if you don't have a book today, in an age when it has never been easier to author a book and instantly reach a global market, you need to get with the times! Your future depends on it.

You must write a book and this book is your blueprint to make this happen—and FAST!

How fast? Get ready to write your 100-page book in less than 12 hours of actual writing time!

Not Everybody Will Fall In Love
With Your Book—But That's Okay

There is a saying that my good friend Stephen Pierce says. Stephen quips, "You'll go broke if you market to all the folk; you'll grow rich if you market to a niche."

This book will show you how to find the market that is hungry for your attitudes, skills and knowledge. Just ASK™ is the acronym I use in my speaking engagements, workshops, teleseminars and keynotes. You will realize that in order to grow rich, you must with laser precision focus on the specific desires of a specific group of people. In other words, you must communicate your expertise to a very defined group or target audience, herein referred to as your target market.

The New Dynamic Duo

Tie your passion into what your target market wants and make a difference in the lives of others globally. In fact, think like a savvy marketer—which this book will teach you—and grow rich as an expert.

Your Book Is Your Sales Brochure

Robert Kiyosaki, author of the **Rich Dad Poor Dad** series held up his book at a recent conference and declared, "This is my number one sales brochure." Your book will open up the doors for untold opportunities and it all begins with your book.

Your Book Positions You As The Expert

I know what many of you are thinking. I would love to write a book about _____ but there are already so many other people who already have written about this. Don't worry. When you understand this basic marketing principle you will realize that you can never satiate the thirst for a want. And of course, this book will help you differentiate yourself so that you never have to worry about your competitors! Why? Because I will help you ensure that your material is uniquely yours. And I will help you communicate this to your target market.

Don't worry.

First of all, no one is going to have your unique experiences. Second, I firmly believe that you cannot really put a dollar value on the demand of something in the market place if you learn how to position your book properly. This book will help do this for you.

As I will show you later on, learning and teaching comprise three fundamental components: attitudes, skills and knowledge...That's why I say "Just ASK™" at my live speaking engagements.

Nothing establishes your expertise like authoring your own book, and with today's technology, it has never been easier. This is especially true when you have an opportunity to work with a mastermind team who will lead you step-by-step through the process. Go now to find if there are any spaces and if you qualify to work directly with my world class team of award winning authors, editors and business building team. Please note there is usually a waiting list so please be patient if seats are filled.

Visit http://AuthorAndGrowRich.com/bonuses/rich for more information on the **Entrepreneurial Authoring Program,** which consists of the Mastermind Program or the Home Study Course. Experience what it is like to have an entire team working with you for 6 months to answer your questions, help you personalize the material in this book and help you create your Internet business as you author your book. You will discover the same principles that I have used to set two Internet records.

Your Book Is The Key To Leaving Your Legacy

Ben Franklin stated, "If you want to be remembered well after you pass away, either write things worth reading or do things worth writing." Ben Franklin realized the power of a written legacy.

Prove Right Now That You Have What It Takes To Become A Successful Author With This Assessment Tool

Download the

Entrepreneurial Authoring Assessment Plan,

a bonus ($17 Value) for you from the following URL...

(FREE BONUS $17 Value)

http://AuthorAndGrowRich.com/bonuses

This assessment tool has been created to help you analyze the specific attitudes, skills and knowledge that you will use in the authoring process.

Download the **eBARQ**, the eBook Authoring Readiness Quotient, another special bonus for you ($17 Value), which is a powerful assessment tool to help you analyze what is

I know you have what it takes...it's time for YOU to realize this once and for all.

(FREE BONUS $17 Value)
http://AuthorAndGrowRich.com/bonuses

Your Book Is The Key To Automated Wealth Thanks To The Power Of The Internet

The Internet is the best real estate today. I didn't say this, but Mark Victor Hansen, author of the mega best-selling series, **Chicken Soup For The Soul** did. If the Internet is the best real estate today, then your digital book is your ocean front property.

Now, the key to selling your book on the Internet with profit margins of well over 90% is to first create it as a digital product and then release it as a "hard" copy version.

If you don't think people read electronic books, called digital books or more commonly eBooks, you're wrong. The International Digital Publishing Forum reported a 23% increase in eBook (electronic book) revenue in 2005 over 2004. Digital publishing is, indeed, on the rise.

But how do you produce your book as a digital product, then get it published in print?

The great news is that this book is going to teach you about publishing it first as a digital book or an electronic book. After that, you'll be in a position to get your manuscript into print. **Author And Grow Rich** not only teaches you how to write a book in only 12 hours of actual writing time, but enables you to gain instant access to a New York Publisher without submitting a proposal, experiencing countless rejections, or sharing profits with an agent. Who and how?

How To Gain Instant Access To A New York Publisher

This book will show you how to gain instant access to a New York Publisher. That's right! You will not only be shown how to get your book finished in record time and get it on the Internet to sell faster than you have ever dreamed possible, but the greatest news is this: you will receive through the Entrepreneurial Authoring Program, which consists of the Mastermind Program and the Home Study Course, instant access to our New York Publisher.

What Is Entrepreneurial Authoring And Publishing?

The basis of these programs offered by AwakenTheAuthorWithin.com is to help each author think and act like a business person. The way to achieve true freedom in life is to operate your own business. And these programs ensure the following:

1. Your book is built on the back of a solid foundation: a target market that already wants what you have before you even begin to write!

2. You will know the profit potential of your book/business idea.

3. Your book will act as a high powered sales force, a 20th Century business card demonstrating your expertise and positioning you as an industry expert. It truly is the most powerful lead generation system today.

4. Your book will be the champion for other product and services that you offer

5. Your book published in both electronic and print book versions will garner you the highest profit margins, greatest exposure and help you achieve the wealth so that you can do what you have always wanted to do.

Authoring A Book, Even Though I Came Close To Flunking High School English, Is How I Found My Life!

There is a power that can only be felt when you put your thoughts on paper. That is why you should write your own book and not have someone else ghost write it. As soon as you put something down on paper, you own it! It is yours. No one else has ever framed a thought as you have. Think about that! At ThePersonYouMustBecome.com we teach that writing is also the quickest way to connect with your emotional self. In order to achieve your emotional freedom to become the person that you must become, you should write to facilitate this connection.

Writing Is The Doing Part Of Thinking

What is the fastest way to make changes in your own life? Write! Why is this? Because when you are through with a writing session, your conscious brain can now go to sleep, but more importantly, your unconscious mind is now awakened. Your unconscious mind is where you do up to 90% of your thinking. It is where problems are solved. The trouble is that few people access their subconscious minds to solve their problems.

But not you! With this book, you will get help to train your mind and develop habits to utilize your subconscious mind so that you solve all the problems that your audience will have. You see, few people do this and this is why authoring using the **Author and Grow Rich** model is so potent. You will clearly see for yourself the power of becoming a solution provider.

A fundamental teaching method to help students learn material faster than what they ever thought possible is to incorporate into the learning environment as many modalities as possible. These different modalities include sight, sound, touch and taste. The process of writing is a kinesthetic behavior that facilitates the incorporation of the subconscious mind to process what you have written. In short, when you write you can't help but change your life.

The Internet Is How I Discovered Freedom

Several years ago I was living other people's dreams for my future. I was the youngest Vice Principal of my school board and many people had me slated as the next Superintendent and Director of Education. That was my goal, I thought. Until my wife, Fiona, literally kicked me out of our home. Why?

Well, with two post graduate degrees, I was intent on going for my PhD.

Go South-West Young Man

Armed with a few of Robert Kiyosaki's **Rich Dad Poor Dad** books, Fiona sent me to California to visit with a friend. What made this trip so memorable is that we had absolutely no money. In fact, that Christmas, we did not give our children any presents as we simply could not afford any. Yet my beloved wife purchased an airline ticket for me so that I could get away and find out what I really wanted to do with my life.

The Age Of Information Marketing Is Over

Where do people go when they have a problem? The Internet. This is where you should start...Get your book online.

We are drowning in information. The Internet's greatest advantage, which has been leveling the playing field so now everybody with a computer and an Internet connection has access to the same information. It has also become your greatest annoyance. Today we are drowning in information. We are over-communicated to.

You know what I mean.

The Age Of Recommendation Marketing Is Here

We used to live in the Information Age, but you know how it goes when everyone jumps on the bandwagon... We both know that everyone is glutted with more information than we know what to do with. You surf the web and there is page after page of information, right? But how do you sort and sift through it all and solve your problems?

That is why we are at the dawn of a new age: The Recommendation Age. People don't want information. They want solutions to their problems, and that means they need information filtered through the expertise of someone who has gone before them. And that's going to be YOU when you write your book.

Joe Vitale puts it this way: "What people want is not more data, numbers, facts and figures. What people want is what all that information is supposed to provide: a way to make their lives happier, easier, fuller and more satisfying...They want to be taken by the hand by a trusted, knowledgeable source and led to wealth, freedom, enrichment, salvation, eternal happiness...Whatever it is they truly and deeply desire."

Your Life Experiences and Passion position you with the natural readiness to make recommendations to others. You do it all the time in small ways. Think about it. Haven't you ever told a friend—or even a stranger—to steer clear of a product that doesn't live up to expectations? Haven't you ever suggested a tasty dish at a restaurant, or told a friend why she would absolutely love a movie you just saw? I know you have. We all do this. It's time to cash in on a natural human tendency. It's time for YOU to write your book. And you bought this book because you want guidance through that process, right?

That's The Power Of Recommendation Marketing.

What will you recommend? How to solve other people's problems. The type of writing that sells the best on the Internet, as you will see, is non-fiction. People want help solving their problems. In **The Long Tail**, author Chris Anderson demonstrates the power of the Internet and how it has allowed any market, no matter how small, to become profitable, especially when you understand the fundamental skills of sales and marketing we are going to teach you in this book.

I Have Great News For You!

Have you ever dreamed of writing a book? Have you ever dreamed of leaving a written legacy? Have you wanted to access the power of the Internet to reach a global market with your passion?

Remember I told you that according to statistics, 83% of people in America want to write a book. This is a dream of most people. Yet, what is very disturbing is that few people have taken action on their dream. Back on page 1 I shared with you specific reasons why this happens.

But this isn't you! I want you to open up your life to a world of possibilities. Before you apply the skills needed for success in life, you must first position your mind.

Every author in the world is capable of authoring a 100 page book in less than 12 hours of actual time. Read on and find out how YOU can be next. It's your turn.

Remember this important fact: the information age is dead. We're drowning in information. What people want now is for an expert to recommend a solution. The Recommendation Age is here. Take your place as an expert and cash in on the Recommendation Age by writing YOUR book—starting now!

GLENN DIETZEL

CEO, Awakened, LLC
http://www.AwakenTheAuthorWithin.com

You've Always Dreamed Of Writing A Book

A large box arrives from a New York Publisher. It's here—YOUR BOOK! You hurriedly rip it open and take the first book out. There it is...YOUR NAME as the author of your first book. You forget to breathe and your heart skips a beat in excitement.

You caress the spine and read the title and your very own name again. The cover looks great. You read the back cover and study it carefully. Even though you saw the proofs, it's like you've never seen it before. Your excitement builds. There is nothing like the thrill of holding a book you authored in your hands—except the exhilaration of growing rich because of the business you build around it!

You hold the book and feel its heft in your hands. All your hard work ... researching the needs of your intended audience...reading about other books in your topic...looking for the needs that only you can fill ... writing your book...creating "buzz" in your book before it ever made it into print...has paid off.

You hold the book to your nose and smell it. There is nothing like that new book aroma of paper and ink—when you're the AUTHOR!

Who will you tell first? Your spouse? Your best friend? Your mother? Or maybe the person or people who tried to squash your dream? You made your big dream come true despite all the negativity the dream-stealers could throw at you.

Because of everything you learned in the **Author and Grow Rich** program, your book is already creating a stir on the Internet and around the world. You are receiving offers to do interviews, be a guest on podcasts, and appear on live broadcasts. You are getting hit after hit on your website because you have wisely peppered the net with your articles and special offers. You are becoming the go-to expert in your area...

And you are helping thousands and thousands of people solve their problems...

And your book is getting lots and lots of attention...

And you are growing a thriving business...

And you are growing RICH!

If this is your dream, read this book and more importantly, take action on the material covered on the following pages and your dream will become your reality.

Book Now For Your
Free Consultation Call (Value $500)

Here is what to do first. Phone our office at (519)542-3043 to set up an appointment so that we can help you specifically personalize the material in this book for your specific circumstance. We will provide you specific action steps to help you with finding your passion, the positioning of your idea in the market place and help you to drive traffic to your website where you will sell your book.

I know you have just the answers a hungry market is looking for.

Internet marketer and affiliation expert Ken McArthur wanted to write the seminal guide to creating a huge impact in the world. When his proposal was accepted by a major New York Publisher, he needed a system that would teach him to fast write his book to meet a deadline less than four months away. He is the first author to be coached live to a worldwide audience by Glenn and the Awakened Team.

Join his free membership community at http://www.TheImpactFactor.com and buy his book *Impact: How to Get Noticed, Motivate Millions, and Make a Difference in a Noisy World* at any bookstore.

$$$ AUTHOR AND GROW RICH $$ CHECKLIST

How To Write Your Book In 12 Hours Of Actual Writing Time

PRE-WRITING CHECKLIST

- ❏ Book Title and Sub-title

- ❏ Target Market Analysis

- ❏ Target Market Description

- ❏ Problems of the Target Market—and Solutions

- ❏ Benefits and Features of the Book

- ❏ USP - Unique Selling Proposition

- ❏ MSP - Multiple Selling Propositions

- ❏ UPP - Unique Personal Proposition

THE ACTION PLAN

- ❏ Book Genealogy Tree™—Chapters

- ❏ Chapter Titles

- ❏ Individual Chapter Genealogy Trees™

12 Hours Of Actual Writing Time Using The Individual Chapter Genealogy Trees™

POST-WRITING CHECKLIST

❑ Research and Add Additional Information

❑ Organize the Chapter Content Using Delivery Options e.g. Q & A; Case Studies

❑ Add Graphics, Charts, Photographs, Clip Art...

❑ Edit the Text for Flow, Organization, Readability...

❑ Proof-read for Spelling, Grammar, Syntax, Active-Passive voice...

❑ Write Additional Pages e.g. TOC, Copyright/Legal, Appendix, Contact, Sales...

❑ Add Hyperlinks—Internal and External

❑ Format Pages For ePublishing

THE PUBLISHING

❑ ePublish As A PDF File And then Awakened Submits Your Manuscript Directly To Our New York Publisher!

CELEBRATE!

How To Write A 100 Page Book In 12 Hours Of Actual Writing Time

E very author is capable of writing a 100 page book in 12 hours of actual writing time. The **Author and Grow Rich** book addresses several concerns of authors as they embark on their book authoring journey.

You Need To Know Where You Are Going!

This summative checklist indicates the necessary steps in the authoring process both pre-writing and post-writing. This is where you are going—your plan of action.

The Pre-Writing Checklist and The Action Plan lay the groundwork for the writing.

The 12 Hours of Actual Writing Time using the Individual Entrepreneurial Authoring Genealogy Tree™ system (refer to chapter 4) uses the pre-writing preparation a matter of using the Entrepreneurial Authoring Genealogy Tree™ information as your outline for your writing. Once you get to this stage of writing, the ideas will flow form your detailed outline. No writer's block here! Write from the heart—edit with the mind. Put pen to paper or fingers to keyboard and just write—write—write! Once you start writing the difficulty will be in stopping. The book will flow out of you!

When the draft version of your book is completed, your Post-Writing Checklist is applied. At this point in the authoring process your book is written but requires the finishing touches to turn a manuscript into a book ready for publication.

The Publishing is the transformation of your final draft of the book into an Adobe Acrobat—PDF document maximizing the book technology available to book authors.

Instant Access To A New York Publisher

Once you have gone thru our Entrepreneurial Authoring Program which consists of the Mastermind Program or the Home Study Course and you have published electronically, that means you have published your manuscript as an eBook, AwakenTheAuthorWithin.com will submit your book directly to our New York Publisher. And what's more, you retain the rights to your manuscript! This is an industry first!

Celebrate needs no explanation! Congratulations!

You Need To Know Where You Have Been!

Authors can make use of this summative checklist in other ways. As they progress through the book authoring process the checklist is visualization of what has been accomplished. It ensures you have done everything you should have done to become a successful book author. This summary checklist is used during the process to track progress.

You Need To Know Where To Go To Find The Information!

The summary is also a quick reference to the chapters relevant to the content. The **Author and Grow Rich** summary is divided into 5 working sections: Pre-Writing Checklist; The Action Plan; 12 Hours of Actual Writing Time; Post-Writing Checklist; and finally The Publishing Phase.

The order of completion of each item within each of these sections isn't important. But completion of all steps in each section is imperative. To assist you in locating the relevant information for each step on the checklist use the convenient chapter reference.

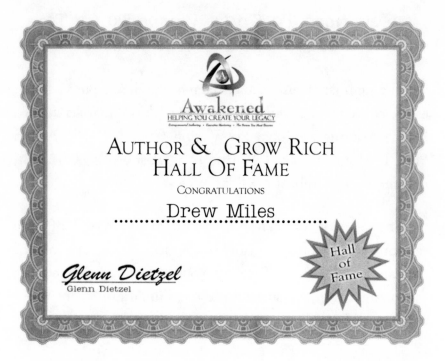

Drew Miles, "The Wealth-Building Attorney" had his book manuscript sitting in a drawer for a couple of years. He had the idea, the basic structure, but did not have the time or the know-how to complete and market his book, so he came to Glenn Dietzel. His book, **Zero to Success: 10 Keys to Creating a Very Profitable Business by Legally Keeping More of What You Make** launched last fall. He has boosted his credibility tremendously. He launched a coaching program and a speaking business around this book and now can say that he is a published author.

See his book at http://zero2success.com/

Are you wondering

whether or not you have

what it takes to author

a book?

Read on...

CHAPTER

How To Create

The Mindset Of A

Tiger Woods, A Bobby Fischer

And A Robin Williams...All In One!

The Internet Marketplace

Three Major Reasons People Come To The Internet:

1. To make money or save money

2. To find solutions to problems

3. To find happiness and fulfillment

Top 10 Niche Markets Today On The Internet Based On My Research Working With Clients Over The Past 6 Years

1. To make money or save money

2. Self Help / Personal Development

3. Supernatural / Spiritual

4. Technology / Information Technology

5. Shopping

6. Fitness / Diet

7. Relationships

8. Every Day Problems

9. Food / Recipes

10. Hobbies / Crafts

These markets are so hot they sizzle—BUT you can make big money even if your book is not in one of these areas.

Principles Of Human Nature That You Must Understand Before Authoring Your Money-making book

1. Human nature is a constant. People are driven by the same basic desires and needs as they were hundreds of years ago. And that's a good thing!

2. People buy what they want first and foremost. Making a decision is primarily an emotional one. Then people justify their choice to buy rationally.

Controlling Forces that Drive All Human Action

According to Denis Waitley's **The Psychology Of Winning**, there are two driving forces in human nature. They are:

Pain

Pleasure

According to Robert Collier, one of the all-time great copywriters, these are the 6 major motives for human action:

Love

Gain or Greed

Duty

Pride

Self-Indulgence

Self-Preservation

Joe Karbo, author of **The Lazy Man's Way To Riches** composed this list of 4 major motivators:

Immortality

Recognition

Romance

Reward

Why Start With A Digital Book?

Stats and trends show that online purchases are increasing. In fact, based on the most recent eMarketer.com report, almost 50% of what was purchased in 2004 was purchased on the Internet as this was the only place where this could be purchased.

Four Reasons Why Electronic Public Technology Will Continue To Increase:

1. High profit margins

2. Instant downloads to solve immediate problems

3. Material is current

4. e-Commerce trends.

What Do Others Have To Say?

📖 Mark Victor Hansen, co-creator of the wildly successful **Chicken Soup For The Soul** series, said—"The Internet is the best real estate in the 21st Century"

📖 According to eMarketer.com, the e-publishing industry accounted for $4.1 billion dollars in sales; by the end of 2005, eBooks accounted for 10% of all consumer books. Experts cannot even hazard a guess on what this percentage will be in the next few years or even by the end of this century as technology and consumerism are now integrating more fully.

📖 By the end of 2007, according to a Forrester report, digital delivery of books and related information will generate over 8 billion in sales; in fact 18% of all publishing revenue will be digital downloads.

📖 Consider that in 1993 there were no sales completed on the Internet, by the end of 2003, 42% of what was purchased online was done so because that was the only place where that content could be acquired.

The Internet isn't just for "nerds" anymore. A survey by eMarketer found some interesting statistics. According to their report,

📖 70% of US adults surveyed said they have considered starting their own business.

📖 75% of US adults surveyed believe the Internet has made it easier to start a small business.

📖 80% of small businesses in the US use the Internet to conduct business activities.

Remember that you're not selling information. You're filtering information through your experience to help people solve their problems. You're recommending a course of action. Another report by eMarketer recently stated: "When asked, 75% of consumers said they were most comfortable purchasing a product on the recommendation of a friend."

<u>Conclusion</u>—Ultimately people are willing to pay for content only if it makes them more money, saves them money, or it ties into their career or some other passionate personal interest (according to Rich Gordon, Professor of New Media, Northwestern University).

How To Prepare Your Mind And Recognize Your Areas Of Expertise

The first step in creating a money-making, best-selling book is not what you would think. It is not locking yourself in a closet and demanding peace and quiet. It is not agonizing over what kind of story is going to sell best or when it should be released to capitalize on consumer spending trends.

No, the first and most important step in creating a book is preparing yourself. Any professional athlete or actor will tell you that before the performance comes the preparation. In fact, Dr. Robert Schueller once said that 'spectacular results come from unspectacular preparation'.

Instead of stretching your hamstrings or your quads, you must focus on engaging the most powerful muscle that you possess. It's the one that works 24/7, constantly processing, solving and planning. Of course, it's your mind!

So the question is: "How does one prepare his/her mind for creating a book?" There are a few excellent techniques that we highly recommend.

1. Take a few moments to formulate some questions that you need to have answered. Questions are excellent triggers for the brain to begin thinking because the brain tackles the understanding of the world through questions. The brain thinks in questions and answers. These questions may include: "Why am I writing this book?", "What do I hope to accomplish when it is published?", "What kind of book would be most helpful to my target audience?" etc.

2. Create the proper mindset. What is 'mindset'? Simply put, mindset is the framework that you instruct your mind to act within. It's like telling an actor to read his lines while pretending to be a certain character. Everything that he reads will be done from that character's point of view. In the same way, you must create the mindset of a winner. Tell your brain that you are a winner and your brain will respond accordingly. Internalize the following **25 LEGACY STATEMENTS**. In the next month I want you to memorize them.

25 Statements Of Legacy To Bust Out Of Your Cocoon Of Contentment And Into A World Of Opportunity

These legacy statements provided me the mindset to set two Internet records. As I stated above, they are that powerful that you need to memorize them in the next 30 days. Go to the following URL now and get the 10 minute audio commentary that goes with each.

http://AuthorAndGrowRich.com/bonuses

<u>WARNING</u>: They are incredibly powerful!
(Remember, using them I was able to set two Internet records...and if a former Vice Principal can do this, so can you!)

1. Your Legacy always starts with insignificance.

2. As you move forward out of procrastination, you don't have to get it perfect, you just have to build momentum.

3. Get your Legacy going now; movement builds momentum and permanent habits of success.

4. Feedback is the answer to all your prayers.

5. Always take focused, inspired, outcome-driven action.

6. You have been created to win, but conditioned to lose.

7. You must look within for value, but must look beyond for perspective.

8. Whoever has the strongest focus wins in the market place. Split concentration is why you fail.

9. Your twin tickets to freedom: marketing and sales.

10. Greater sameness will never get you better results.

11. The road to your success is defined by doing things in the order of their importance...by doing what other people do not want to do!

12. The language you use at your weakest moment is the key to driving your success forward.

13. Safety is riskier than you realize. Caution shouldn't be thrown to the wind, but without risks, life isn't an adventure.

14. Always set goals in the context of those ahead of you—the secret to quantum leaps is to think big and do small simultaneously.

15. The closer you get to the goal line...the stronger your resolve must be. Success works on an inverse square formula.

16. You can only see what you know. And what you know must be revealed to you by another person whom you connect with at a heart level.

17. The key to moving forward rapidly is based on the quality and quantity of your pain: the pain of going back must exceed the pain of moving forward.

18. It's not the idea but the presentation of your idea that is the key to your legacy!

19. He or she who self reflects the greatest, leaves the most powerful legacy.

20. There is never an ideal time to go for your legacy...life will never stop!

21. The only dichotomy you must feel to know you are going for your legacy: excitement and fear.

22. Information is passive; knowledge is active; wisdom is dominance.

23. You must have a mentor and mastermind team!

24. Public accountability is the greatest form of motivation!

25. The power of your legacy is defined by your willingness to challenge the ordinary of each moment.

How else do you get your winning mindset? Here are a few more tips! Successful people do not focus on dotting all the 'I's'

and crossing all the 'T's.' They know that to start out, you need ideas, not critiques! You need to be writing, not editing! So they focus on writing with their hearts and save the 'editing with their minds' for much later. Too many people get hung up on all the details and lose the motivation to act. One of my mentors always told me, "You don't have to get it right, you just have to get it going!"

Creativity is found in the subconscious mind. That is why a solution cannot be solved with the same process that created it in the first place. Writing is a creative act, and successful authoring must come from your subconscious.

The Business Mindset

Business is about influence, or "leverage." Your book is a tool to leverage your credibility. And the first step in preparing your mind for success is to see yourself as an expert. Another way of looking at this is that you must sell yourself first to your dream of the possibility of becoming a money-making book author.

So there are really two sales that must take place: the first sale is the one you make to yourself. The second sale is the one that actually produces money for you when your target market completes the transaction with you.

To master the sale to yourself it is imperative that you write your own book. No ghost writer. You want your voice to come out strong and clear. One of the concepts we will discuss is your UPP which stands for your Unique Personal Proposition. And there is nobody better to get your message out then you! No one else has your story. And remember that the main reason that people come to the Internet is to solve problems. The purchasers of your book want your guidance. So you are paid to provide solutions to the problems that keep people up at night.

The Internet Is The Embodiment Of The Information Age

However, in a day and age of information overload you are not paid to deliver content. Your book puts content in the context of your expert guidance. This is an important distinction and one that bears some time to discuss.

Content is merely that...information devoid of context, floating around in nothing. And when we speak of context, we are speaking of your target audience's needs and wants. You need to be able to feel their pain and show your intended audience that you understand what they are going through.

Denis Waitley in his book, **Winning the Innovation Game**, has this to say about this crucial distinction: "If you are an entrepreneur or knowledge worker, and as an author you definitely fit this description. Your success depends on how well you think. You are not paid to collect, sort, store or retrieve information, although you may do all of these things. You are paid to interpret that information and to create and implement new ideas."

How To Create A Winning Idea

Here is how you create ideas: Complete a five minute exercise where you list as many ideas that are related to what you want to do. The key is to write everything down and do not pre-judge anything. This is the creative phase and you want to write as quickly as you can. Do not reflect at all on your ideas. The personal reflection comes in the next phase.

The key to brainstorming and recording all your ideas is that it allows your subconscious to begin to find relationships among your ideas. There are three relationships that your mind will look at when analyzing your ideas. The great philosopher Socrates first espoused this concept over 2300 years ago. It involves your mind analyzing a) the similarity of your ideas (What are your ideas like?); b) The contiguity of your ideas (How are your ideas related to each other?); and c) the contrasting nature of your ideas (How are your ideas different?).

The ideas you create should all be involved in solving your target market's problems. To bring this home on how this should impact the creation of your book, the late and great G.K. Chesterton summarizes the importance of analyzing problems first when he stated that the focus should not be on your book, but on understanding and magnifying your target market's problems first.

This begins with understanding the difference between empathy and sympathy. As a money-making book author who wants to build a profitable business because of your book, you must empathize with your target market. Empathy goes one step further than sympathy, though the difference is essentially one of focus. Sympathy is the ability of showing how sorry you are that one person is going through a painful situation. Empathy focuses on providing solutions for your target market. And the solutions that you provide should communicate the desired attitudes (what should I think) and the specific skills that are required to move to the desired end point (How do I get what I want and why should I do it a certain way and how do I implement an overall strategy in my life to make it happen).

Implementation is a key reason why information is the enemy to ultimate success. Information is passive as it fails to contextualize content. In fact, analyze what happens when you want to solve a problem. You begin studying an area to solve your problem such as repairing a vacuum cleaner. What happens is that when you begin to analyze a subject devoid of any reference point, you begin to realize what you don't know. What happens is that you begin to acquire a vast amount of information not really knowing what you need to know to solve the problem. This leads to you acquiring a lot of non useable information. The end result is that you are not able to take focused action as you have no frame of reference from which to take action.

The Author's Mindset

The first principle is preparation. Authoring your money-making book is no different than preparing to participate in an athletic event. You don't just show up on game day without putting your body through immense preparations. The key to authoring a money-making book is to prepare to write your money-making book.

Here are the steps in preparation as we see it: there must be order in your life...this begins in your mind and then must be channeled with a concrete game plan. Your success must acknowledge the need for patience, endurance and the ability to act in the face of fear and failure.

The First Step In Preparation
Is To Acknowledge Your Dream.

The Second Step Is To
Take Action On Your Dream Of
Authoring Your Money-making Book.

This book is about the necessary mindset and the actions that you must take to make this happen.

Look in your heart, for out of it proceeds the important issues of life.

The reason most people who take the time to acknowledge their dream of authoring a money-making book fail to make it happen is because of one of the "deadly characteristics of resistance." This will require you to ignore immediate gratification in favor of long term commitment to completing your book. Successful people focus on the future and on the reward of accomplishing a difficult task; unsuccessful people focus on the present moment refusing to move out of their comfort zone to challenge themselves to accomplish their dreams. This latter group of people resist in the moment that could take them toward their dream.

What is resistance? Great question! Let's start by saying that change requires diligence, persistence, and a willingness to do what you need to do one step at a time, every day, whether you're "in the mood" or not. Resistance comes in forms like, "I'm so busy today," or "I'm too tired to work on my book," or "I just have too much going on in my life right now," or "I'll start tomorrow."

We become too accustomed to getting things fast. Microwave ovens deliver dinner in minutes. Fast food is available all over town. The Internet means we can do business any time of the day or night. This isn't all bad, but it can lead to an over-reliance on instant results.

What you hold in your hands is as close to an instant book as you can possibly get. I've created a system for you to follow so you can be successful. Yes, you do have to apply yourself, but all you have to do is follow the path I've set before you one step at a time. This book is about decreasing the time it will take you to personally experience the gratification of a completed book. Immediate gratification in this case is about the feeling you will experience once your money-making book is completed.

But I know you will have to deal with one ugly reality in order to make your dream a reality. What lies between immediate gratification and authoring a book that you must confront if you are to succeed in this endeavor? You guessed it...Resistance.

Perhaps you think that what holds you back is completely outside yourself, in the form of busy schedules and hectic lives, but that's not the problem. Here is the genius about resistance: it does not exist outside oneself. It exists as a wall that lies between where you are currently and where you see yourself...as a money-making author. The subtle power of resistance is the fact that it lies not outside of you, but **within you**!

The strength of resistance is in direct proportion to the strength of your calling. In other words, the bigger your dream, the more internal "junk" you have to overcome to make it happen. As stated above, everyone has a desire to leave a written legacy. It is part of being human! And since this hard-wired desire is such an intimate activity that involves your very self, the conflict is enormous.

The ugly face of resistance is procrastination. Author Steven Pressfield in his book, **The War of Art: Break Through the Blocks and Win Your Inner Creative Battles**, defines procrastination "as the ease to which we tend to rationalize our lack of taking action." This makes it all the more seductive. We don't tell ourselves, "I'm not going to write my money-making book." No, instead we state, "I am going to write my money-making book; and I am going to do it tomorrow."

Tomorrow. The ultimate face of resistance. And the strength of this learned behavior is that it enslaves us to believe that someday everything will be right for us to begin the process, as if life will suddenly stop and God will write in the clouds that you should begin now!

So how do you know it is your time? By the simple fact that you are unhappy with not moving forward. And here is another test. You know procrastination is dominating your life when you experience the feeling of complete emptiness after you give in to all the things you do for immediate gratification.

Two Important Attitudes to Consider...

Have you ever analyzed why you have felt upset or disgruntled with people? Maybe you have even caught yourself criticizing others? What is the root cause of criticizing others that are living their Big Dream? It's simply the fact that they are being true to their big dream while we are not.

Another attitude that seems almost counter-intuitive to success is self-doubt. Self-doubt really is your friend? Why? Because it demonstrates that you are really going after the Big Dream of authoring a book. It reflects your purpose, your passion, and your love of what is found in one's heart.

Here is another attitude that on the surface appears to be an enemy of success: fear. The fact that you are fearful demonstrates that subconsciously you must do what scares you: in this case, author a book!

Here is an interesting consideration about fear: fear can never be overcome. The secret is to act in spite of your fear for the successful author knows that once you begin taking action, your fear will subside.

And this action must happen each day. This book is your action-driven road map to slaying resistance and propelling yourself forward with a game plan to ensure your success on two levels. This begins with success first at the belief level (your attitude) and secondly at the "please show me exactly what I must do to implement a successful strategy to complete my book." (And with this system, you will author a book that will allow you to become the instant expert in less than 12 hours of actual writing time!)

Thirty-Seven Secret Ways To Make Your Brain Get The Write Idea

Now you have successfully engaged your mind. It is time to put it to work with some writing exercises. Here are 37 different tips to help your brain get the 'WRITE' idea:

1. When an idea comes to you, usually unexpectedly, it is time to write ¾ right now! Record it on anything that's handy and transfer it to full size paper or onto your computer as soon as possible so you won't lose it.

2. You should write as long and as often as possible when you're "in the mood" to write. Ideas can flow over a period of minutes, hours and days so steal time if you have to in order to write when you are on a roll. It's a justifiable action.

3. Write in the places where you are most inspired and where you go to relax and rejuvenate yourself. If you write in these places you will increase writing time because these are the places you frequent often in order to make sense of life. Inspirational locations bring out the best in you.

4. Carry with you at all times key words and phrases from your Table of Contents along with supporting points you want included. Use this barebones outline to write in the waiting rooms of doctors' offices or while your wife/husband is shopping or whenever the opportunity presents itself. Key words and phrases is all you need to get you started writing. It's all the inspiration you need.

5. Get up a little early 2 or 3 days a week or go to bed a little later 2 or 3 days a week setting aside this time to write. You might also consider using part of your lunch hour, if you get an hour, to write a few days a week.

6. If you are a sports fan write between periods, at half time or even during those 3-5 minute commercial breaks. You might also try keeping the sports event on the TV 'muted' even when the game is on. If I'm rolling along with my writing I don't really need the sound to understand what is going on and I can always un-mute the TV if something interesting is going on.

7. If you're writing a particularly interesting or important section of your book, leave it out where you can see it. It's easier to just pick it up and write for a few minutes if it's readily available. It also generates ideas just by looking at it and you can jot down those ideas in the margins of your work. (In our house my papers may get moved in the tidying process. Make sure you know where your spouse puts those tidied papers!)

8. Arrange to exchange babysitting or child watching sessions with someone to allow you to write in a large block of time when it's your best time to write. I'm a morning writer and a sports watching writer. I also love writing in coffee shops! Exchanging child sitting time must be mutually beneficial. Using this kind of arrangement also removes any guilt and frustration you might have in finding and using large blocks of time.

9. Pay someone to look after the children. At crucial times in the book authoring process this may be a good investment. This is especially true if writing is a recreational activity for you. You deserve time for yourself doing what you want to do that has a positive impact on your life.

10. Request for your birthday a weekend retreat to write your book. Pick a location that's inspiring for you, relaxing but not distracting, and where interruptions are at a minimum. It could be at a friend's house or cottage while they are away for the weekend. Or better yet, send your family away on a great weekend vacation while you stay at home in the comfort of your own office. This plan works just as well for a single day as it would for a weekend.

11. Treat the time you take for writing as "recreational" time. It's writing time that energizes you and makes your life more worthwhile. Tell others how important writing time is for you. They will help you find time to write.

12. Make a pact with your spouse or significant other to trade large blocks of time so each of you can pursue your individual interests. This removes any conflicts and any guilt feelings about using large blocks of time for writing.

13. Prioritizing is a key to successfully reaching your goals in life. Making writing one of your priorities and advertising that priority of yours will open up possibilities to write more. Others respect what you value if they value your friendship.

14. Think Big Picture. Your daily "to-do list" cannot govern your life. Authoring a book is a Big Picture item. Taking time out just to think and reflect and plan is okay. It will motivate you to write. Go for a bike ride or a walk in the woods to help you keep focused on the Big Picture. Remember that writing is the doing part of thinking. Give yourself time to think and reflect.

15. Set specific measurable goals regarding time to write. Schedule two 1.5 hour blocks of writing time each week for example, after considering the impact on others and accommodating your schedule. Writing daily for 15 minutes each day may be a reasonable and attainable goal.

16. Take 15 minutes a day as reflective time or I.G.A. time (Idea Generating Activity Time). Think about what you are working on and record all ideas that come to you during this time. In this situation you are writing ideas not content but the content will come later.

17. Invite your friends to have coffee and treats with you. Tell them in advance you want their input on some ideas you have for your book. Pay for their coffee and "harvest" their ideas. This motivates you to write and enhances your commitment to the process. Remember that reflection and I.G.A. activities are an integral part of the writing process.

18. Get a buddy. A writing buddy! Buddies are like mentors —only better. Buddies are friends. Commit to specific writing and reflecting time with your buddy. Choose a buddy who is also writing a book. Time spent with this buddy will translate into more and better writing time and new and better ideas.

19. Write when you need to! Drop everything and write when the time is right or the situation demands it. Don't feel guilty! You can forgo other jobs and responsibilities you should have been doing and do them later. If others can do this then why can't you?

20. Use your time more efficiently by having all the materials you need for writing located in one location so you can just sit down at any time and write. Whenever you end one writing session you should automatically prepare the catalyst material to begin the next. This includes being very specific about the topic and key words to begin writing immediately upon sitting down. You will save 10 to 15 or more minutes per session when you prepare in advance. Take 5 minutes to get ready at the end of each writing session to prepare for the next one, and save writing time for the next session.

21. Making writing appointments with yourself in your personal planner or PDA will ensure you get some writing done. Often what gets written down gets done and your writing time is no exception.

22. Establish realistic time lines for long-range goals. View target dates with flexibility in mind. Be prepared to change direction temporarily if circumstances dictate it. Three 30-minute writing sessions may be more realistic than one session of 1.5 hours. By putting undo pressure on yourself you will act in a counter-productive manner in terms of finding time to write.

23. If you are watching television and the show is not really capturing your interest, take that time to write. If you have materials readily available and organized then shifting your attention to writing rather than watching won't be a problem. This applies equally well to other activities that aren't capturing your interest.

24. You write more effectively and efficiently by taking regular breaks during long writing sessions. Taking breaks is using your time wisely. The breaks allow the sub-conscious to take over and generate new ideas. Make sure you record these brilliant ideas!

25. Take one lunch hour per week. Eat a "quickie" lunch and use the time to write. Is there a library or quiet spot near your workplace where you can go? Is writing in your car out of the question? What about staying at your desk while others are away having lunch?

26. If you commute to work by train or bus or car pool, you can use that time to write. Perhaps you can car pool once or twice a week so you can write during the trip. Make sure your car-pooling partners are aware of what you want to do during the commute. On vacation trips or other long drives, write while your spouse drives. Drivers are usually content to watch the road and concentrate on driving and will not miss your conversation.

27. Be ready to pounce. If a window of opportunity presents itself giving you an opportunity to get some extra writing time, pounce on it. These unscheduled spontaneous writing sessions are often most productive. Appreciate the fact that you must be ready to take advantage of these situations. These are golden opportunities to do something you love to do. Go for it!

28. View your practical every-day writing as an opportunity to hone your writing skills. It's attitude that's important here. Those thank-you notes, staff memos, friendly letters, emails, journal entries and special reports are all writing exercises that give you an opportunity to work on the skills of written communication. You can learn a great deal by writing in all situations. There is always a carry-over to other writing circumstances.

29. Keep writing tools (pen and paper) handy at all times in all places where you just might get the opportunity to write.

30. Writing breeds more writing. The more writing becomes a habit the more it happens. Research says it takes 21 repetitions to break an old habit and establish a new one. Writing for 5-15 minutes per day for 21 consecutive days should establish this writing as a regular habit. So give yourself a reasonable target of 21 repetitions to establish new writing behaviors.

31. Write quickly. Write legibly. Write legible scribbling if necessary. Use abbreviations like "w" for with and acronyms and the first parts of longer words only. If the only person who is going to read your notes is you then take whatever liberties you want to in order to get your ideas on paper and keep the 'flow' going. Scribble now and translate later.

32. As you are writing, put new ideas in the margin of the paper as soon as they come to you. You won't interrupt the flow of your thoughts on the page because you already have some key words to help you and you have already been writing. Slow down to record your new ideas, but don't stop!

33. Use the "Cloze" method of reading for your writing. One technique for teaching students to read is to provide a paragraph with words missing. Students have to fill in the blanks with words suggested by the context of the paragraph. Use this same method to speed up your writing. Insert a straight line in your writing for words that you will know by context when it comes to transcribing your draft copy. Put a _____ in your writing as a placeholder.

34. Use acronyms in your draft copy. You can use the authentic conventional acronyms or you can invent some of your own. For example, "ataw" could mean Awaken The Author Within or "b" for book.

35. Learn to "cover the page". Think in terms of starting every page as if you are going to cover it with writing as quickly as possible with quality ideas. Thinking this way will help you accomplish more writing.

36. Use lists for planning and as content for your book. Lists are important for providing key words under topic headings to get you started writing and to prevent writer's block. Lists: act as a checklist; summarize ideas in a few words; clear the head of ideas; initiate reflective thought; are specific rather than general in nature; are ideas in real words; are useful for personal assessment; spark expansion of ideas; and save writing time. Use lists to keep you organized and to arrange information in your book.

37. Use open-ended statements and questions to keep ideas flowing and to spark new ideas. Write your own stems and questions pertaining to your book content. The more adept you get at writing them the better and faster will be your writing. RaW Stems(tm) are Reflection and Writing open-ended statements requiring brainstorming for ideas to complete the statement.

How To Recognize
Your Areas Of Expertise And Passion

Here are some pointers to help you generate ideas:

1. Define your ideal client.

2. Who are the people you have been working with if you are already in business? What have you liked or disliked about them? Are there any common denominators?

3. What kinds of people could ideally benefit from your knowledge?

4. If you had all the money in the world, what would you be doing?

5. Interview three people you most respect (friends and family members) and ask them what they see you doing? What are your strengths from their standpoint?

6. What have you always been good at?

7. What did you dream of doing as a child?

8. What needs/values do you care about most?

9. Whom do you admire most?

10. What makes you most fulfilled?

11. What do you love to do the most? What are you passionately against?

12. What have you felt called to do?

13. What legacy do you want to leave for your children and grandchildren? What do you want to be remembered for most?

14. Analyze your 'competition' and find out all about them. This will give you ideas as to your niche and how you can brand yourself.

15. Remember that you want to make sure your target market has money to spend.

Two On-going Exercises

1. Produce your own personal inventory. This inventory should be focused on the following:

📖 What you know from the perspective of the attitudes, knowledge and skills you have gained;

📖 Experiences you've had;

📖 Training you have had;

📖 Destinations that you have been to; and

📖 Titles that you have earned.

Create a list of several hundred, even thousands, of descriptors. Note: you will have to keep pen and a pad of paper on you at all times as you will realize all the talents you do have!

Now create a list of "What You Are":

Record a description of yourself. For example, I am a man, father, husband, basketball player, a lover of pizza and Indian food, slightly bald, a resident of Sarnia, Ontario, have four degrees, play the piano, traveler, international speaker, author and creator of the entrepreneurial authoring system etc.

Keep in mind that you want to make sure of two items: 1. The market you are targeting has tremendous wants and desires and 2. The market has money to spend—in other words, it is hungry for your book and other products and services.

Spend some time journaling for a couple of hours. Let it all hang out...write as quickly as you can and get in touch with the real you.

2. Narrow possibilities to two or three. You can do this by playing the devil's advocate with each of your ideas. Provide as many reasons as you can why you shouldn't go with an idea. Now check by completing a focused target market key word analysis on your top two or three ideas.

My top two or three ideas for creating a book and building an online business include _____.

Great! You've started thinking and planning. Time to set your goals and get started on that book!

Awakened
HELPING YOU CREATE YOUR LEGACY

AUTHOR & GROW RICH HALL OF FAME

CONGRATULATIONS

Dr. Simon Evans

Glenn Dietzel
Glenn Dietzel

Hall of Fame

Brain scientist and soccer dad Dr. Simon Evans wanted to write a book that would help parents raise kids with healthy brains who would grow up to become healthy adults. Although he had written countless research papers, his degrees got in the way. One of the biggest challenges he had to overcome was to write in a conversational style so that parents would actually read his book, *Brain Fitness: A Recipe For Feeding Your Child's Dreams And Unlocking Their Maximum Brain Power*. He used key principles from *Author And Grow Rich* as a researcher with the University Of Michigan and finished his book faster than he dreamed possible. He continues to gain more attention for his book and his practical system of healthy living.

Visit Dr. Evans at http://www.BrainFitForLife.com

What else do you need

to get you started?

Read on...

CHAPTER

How To Turn Your Book
Into A SMART Missile That Will
Only Find People
Who Want To Spend Their
Money On YOU.

onsider for a moment what has leveled the playing field in business.

The Internet

With a few key strokes or a push of a button you can have instant access to as much information as you want. Now consider what is perhaps the biggest enemy of the Internet?

Too Much Information!

That's right. It seems like some kind of oxymoron, doesn't it. But consider this. How many times have you gone to the Internet and been absolutely overwhelmed with the volume of information? How many times have you found yourself indecisive about where to go, what to do, and feeling frustrated and by the realization that there is a lot of 'stuff' out there.

Now consider why information is the enemy of your success in executing a winning business plan. What tends to happen when you begin exploring a new topic? If you are like me, you quickly realize what you don't know. And what happens? You begin to spend more time studying and doing research. And here's the problem...I am sure you see it! As you keep studying, you continue to realize how much you don't know. What happens?

Paralysis Of Analysis

Instead of beginning to take action, you continue to glean more and more information.

What You Really Want To Create Is A Knowledge-Based Information Business

Information is your enemy. That's right. Information by itself will prevent you from writing your book and building a successful business quickly...whether it is online or offline. What you want to create for your target market is an 'information' product that incorporates your personal experiences.

Information + Experience = Knowledge

Knowledge + Personal Reflection = Wisdom

What you want your product and service to do is to be a very practical way for your target market to solve their problems. The book you create must be an information product filtered by your experiences that you have learned from the school of hard knocks. If you want your merchandise to really answer your target market's problems, you should provide the opportunity for personal reflection. Your knowledge-based product should provide the ability for your prospect to gain in wisdom. After all, your prospect wants immediate access to what has taken you perhaps years to discover.

📖 Show your prospect what to do= Knowledge

📖 Show your prospect how to do it = Wisdom

Do this successfully, and you will become your prospect's best friend!

Pre-Authoring Readiness
Reflective And Writing Stems—RaW Stems™

The approach I take with this book is to direct you step-by-step as you launch yourself on the Internet with a digitalized book and other products and services. When you commit to taking the Entrepreneurial Authoring Mastermind Mentoring Program, my team and I will walk you through the entire process, every step of the way.

The Reflective and Writing Stems I talk about in this book are tremendous 'starters' that help you prevent writer's block. They are IGAs (see page 59)!

Stems are questions turned into "open-ended" statements.

The statements are then used to generate ideas in a brainstorming fashion. The key is to ask yourself the question that you want answered—which is relatively easy to do—then write it down. After you write the question turn it around to form an open-ended statement. Now write as many answers as possible to complete this statement, accepting any answer that comes to mind.

Once this process is complete, review the brainstormed ideas, accepting and rejecting and refining and choosing the best ones.

Our minds think in questions but create best in statements that give us direction and focus.

Examples:

Question: What were the problems I first faced when I started learning about the topic of my focus?

RaW Stem™: The problems I faced when starting out were...

Question: What are the most important things my readers will need to know to help them solve their problem?

RaW Stem™: At the minimum, my readers will need to know how to...

Question: What is going to be my Unique Selling Proposition (USP) for my book?

RaW Stem™: For my book, I could do one of several things to make my presentation of the material unique enough to draw attention including...

Goals Begin Behavior; Consequences Maintain Behavior!

Introduction

It is ESSENTIAL to set goals, objectives, targets, expected outcomes, etc. throughout the book authoring process. The positive consequences of completing tasks that manifest the goals you have set is the motivation to keep moving forward.

For ease of communication the term 'goals' shall be used to represent all of the synonyms associated with the word.

Big Picture Goals

You must have a general overall goal, which is to write and publish your own book.

This is the BIG PICTURE goal. You need to see yourself weeks from now as a published author collecting 'passive income' for your efforts. Passive income is income generated forever after you have completed the initial book writing. Updates are recommended but not essential. If you choose to provide your book for free you will still receive passive results through your ongoing contribution to someone's successful use of your work. Better still, you could see yourself writing another book.

The big picture goals include some visualizations, some dream fulfillments, some major accomplishment you have always wanted to pursue, and some lasting contribution to a body of knowledge.

Working Goals

Besides the big picture goals, you must establish goals for each of the steps in the book authoring process. These 'working' goals are your nitty-gritty, hard working daily motivators.

Without the big picture goal you won't get started and without the working goals you won't keep going.

We all understand the importance of goals but we're not as good at writing good ones, deciding how to reach them or taking the time to write them down. Even after goals are written, the most important step is often left out. HOW you are going to reach them!

Let's look at a couple of examples:

Big Picture Goals...The Process In Action

June 1, 2008

My goal is to write a book titled, *The Basics of Writing Goals and Objectives* for use by entrepreneurs who want help with focus and execution of their authoring idea. I shall complete the book by June 12, 2008 and be e-published by June 15, 2008.

What Does This Big Picture Goal Have Going For It?

1. It has purpose—talks about the reason for writing and the target audience

2. It is specific—includes a proposed title

3. It is time oriented—time commitments are made in the goal statement

Sounds great so far but you should also:

📖 Write the goal down preferably in a colorful and dramatic fashion and post it in a prominent place where you must read it every day. [Bathroom mirrors?]

📖 Share the goal with as many people as possible but especially with those persons closest to you. This commits you to pursue your goal.

📖 Enlist the support of 2 or 3 people who may not help you write but will encourage you to keep going during the rough times. This allows you to keep progressing toward the goal.

What Next?

Big Picture Goal: to write a book entitled, *The Basics of Writing Goals and Objectives for Entrepreneurs Who Want to Author.*

Start: June 01, 2008—Finish: June 15, 2008

Now you must break that goal down into several sub-goals but still of a general nature.

GOAL	TARGETED FINISH DATE	MEANS TO ACCOMPLISH THE GOAL	ACTUAL FINISH DATE
To write a book in only 12 hours	June 01, 2008	Decide to author a money-making book in 12 hours	
		Contact 2 colleagues or friends to act as mentors	
		Write my big picture goals and share them with my mentors and others	
		Analyze my calendar a minimum of 1 hour per week to author the book	
		Talk to my significant other about what I intend to do and why. Ask for help.	
		Do Target Market Analysis	
		Create Table of Contents	
		Decide on Best Way To Organize Materials	

What Does This Format Of Goal Writing Have Going For It?

1. The big picture (overall) objective is clearly articulated in very specific language.

2. A specific time/date is declared for the completion of each task. THIS IS A MUST!

3. The big picture goal is broken down into WORKING GOALS each one with a targeted completion date.

4. The working goals are also specific and dated.

5. The most important aspect of goal setting and writing is the use of ACTION VERBS to begin each of the means to accomplish the goals. Words such as take, contact, write, gather, set aside, talk,... are CRUCIAL to success.

6. The goals use present tense verbs. There is a 'nowness' about them!

These goals are your action plan. Always write means to accomplish goals beginning with action verbs, the more action the better! Include completion deadlines!

Remember:

"There is doing and not doing.
There is no such thing as trying!"

You can't try to write a book. You have to do something before it really happens.

Working Goals...A Closer Look

This is your first significant step in the authoring process. You have already accomplished at least one of your previous big picture goals...you purchased this book to help you with your desire to become a best-selling author in 12 hours of actual writing time.

Based on the information contained in this book, you must now establish some working goals. Let's take a closer look at working goals. These are the day-to-day goals leading you to completion of the bigger goal of writing your best-selling book in less than 12 hours of actual writing.

Goals re: Completing a Focused Target Market Analysis in Chapter 2, and completing Your Table of Contents (TOC) in Chapter 4.

The format here is only one way this can be done. Do what is most appropriate for you.

(i)   Working goal

(ii) Targeted completion date

(iii) Means to accomplish the goal

(iv) Actual finish date

1. Start working with the material in this book.

June 01   1.1 Download and/or print the information (actual completion date)

June 01   1.2 Skim the information in the book

June 01   1.3 Read information from Chapter One and make brief notes on index cards to that they are on your personhood at all times.

2. Do the work suggested prior to Chapter 1

June 02   2.1 Review the key principles of how to leverage your mind from Chapter One.

June 02   2.2 Email Glenn with your commitment to author a money producing, lead generating book in 12 hours of actual writing

June 02   2.3 Purchase a Dream Journal or better yet, a binder, and keep all your writing collated in this. Keep this on your person at all times so that you remind yourself at all times you are in business authoring your money-making book.

June 02   2.4 Choose and contact my mastermind team members

June 02   2.5 Choose a topic and/or title of my book

3. Start Working on the material in Chapter Two: Complete Your Target Market Analysis.

June 03   3.1 Begin Target Market Analysis

June 03   3.2 Make a list of all your key words and key word phrases using the software at http://www.GoodKeyWords.com

June 03   3.3 Complete the demand for each of your key words and phrases using the Inventory.Overture.com tool

June 03   3.4 Complete the demand related to what advertisers are spending on each of your key words and phrases using http://www.Pixelfast.com

June 03   3.5 Calculate your profit potential for each of your key words or key word phrases http://AuthorAndGrowRich.com/bonuses (You will want to use this software over and over again with other business projects. We use this software with clients and you can get a nice discount as a special valued purchaser of *Author and Grow Rich*.

4. Begin the work on completing the supply (competition) of your authoring idea located in Chapter Two.

And so on...

What Do These Written Goals And Means To Accomplish Them Have To Teach Us?

They are:

📖 Written in specific detail;

📖 Use action verbs;

📖 Positively worded;

📖 Have targeted completion dates; and

📖 Specific to the bigger objective of dealing with the preliminary notes.

In reality, goals are always broken down into smaller and smaller goals again which become the action plan for reaching your big picture goal. They can be added to, revised, have the completion dates altered...so you successfully complete your dream.

BIG PICTURE—the overall goal of writing a book

to

STEPS—also goals but steps/stages/processes/ along the way

to

WORKING GOALS—specific to each of the steps or stages

to

ACTION STATEMENTS—means to accomplish the goals

The 10 Steps To Authoring Your Book

The way we envision it, your best option is to first create an electronic book so that you can start making money AND get feedback before you commit to putting ink to paper through any other publishing option. The following steps are necessary for creating your very first product, the eBook. This is a summary of the book: *The Definitive Guide To eBook Authoring* (Foreword by Dan Poynter). Get the full version here at an incredibly reduced price: Use this book to brainstorm each of the 10 steps in your journey...

http://AuthorAndGrowRich.com/bonuses

As a special bonus and to get a feel of the power of what the above eBook will do in terms of helping you brainstorm ideas for each step of your authoring/business adventure, here is an un-announced bonus for you...

Step Descriptor
RaW Stems™ [Reflective and Writing Stems]

I Idea

📖 I've always dreamed about writing a book about _____ .

📖 My experience says a book about _____ is needed.

📖 If I wrote a book about _____, _____ would be interested in it.

II Reflection

📖 My primary motivation for authoring a book is _____.

📖 Additional benefits to writing it will be _____.

📖 I have a head start on the process because _____.

III Commitment

📖 I will discuss the book concept with _____.

📖 I will seek out additional information about books from _____.

📖 I will sign up for a book authoring and mentoring course from _____.

IV Big Picture

📖 In general terms my book will be about _____.

📖 Some of the topics covered in my book will be _____ .

📖 The objectives of the book will be to _____.

V Chunking

📖 The general topic will have sub-topics such as _____ .

📖 The format(s) I choose to use will include _____.

📖 In terms of portability, interactivity, and versatility I will _____.

VI Writing

📖 The choice of word processor, font, graphics...will be _____.

📖 My style of writing shall be _____

📖 In this part of the process, I shall seek help from _____.

VII Editing

📖 After writing with flow and little editing I will be ready to _____.

📖 I will use automatic spell and grammar checking as well as _____.

📖 Since this is a time-consuming and crucial step I shall _____.

VIII Publishing

📖 Among the choices I have for publishing I choose _____ because _____.

📖 The eye appeal of my book is ensured by _____.

📖 The publishing process is _____.

IX Marketing

📖 I shall choose _____ for marketing my book because _____.

📖 In addition to the primary marketer I shall _____ to sell my book.

📖 To track my book on the market I shall _____.

X Celebrating

📖 After completion of the book I plan to _____.

📖 I shall send thank-you's and copies of my book to _____.

📖 Upon reflection of the book authoring process I intend _____.

Idea

📖 Another book is on the way!

As a Special Bonus, download the following eBook, **10 Simple Steps to eBook Authoring** ($27 Value) from the following URL...

(FREE BONUS $27 Value)

http://AuthorAndGrowRich.com/bonuses

REVIEW YOUR GOALS

WHY?

📖 A progress report toward your dream

📖 Keeps you motivated and working

📖 Justifies the process of goal setting

📖 Keeps you on track with your time lines

📖 Gives you cause to celebrate

WHEN?

📖 At regular intervals during the process [weekly, bi-weekly, monthly]

📖 At the end of each step along the way

📖 When you need a boost by seeing what you've already accomplished

📖 When you reflect on past goals.

📖 When you re-write or add goals.

HOW?

📖 Set aside a specific time to review goals [Sunday evening before you begin your new week)

📖 Write a journal note about your progress

📖 Tell someone about what you are doing.

📖 **Then celebrate again!** You can never get enough celebrating!

Goals are powerful. They are the fuel that keeps you going as you work toward your dream.

Next, you'll discover the secret desires and needs that will empower you to satisfy the readers who are hungry for what only you can feed them.

Wes Waddell was able to leave his systems engineering job and run his business with his wife Kathy full time because he discovered the power of having their own book. He loves that short commute past the coffee pot into the office, and he knows firsthand that having a book helps not only the credibility of your business, but your personal credibility as well. Today Wes has created the Internet's largest membership scrap booking site.

Visit Wes at http://www.PrincessCrafts.com.

Do you just want to

write a book—or do you

want to build an

information empire?

Read on...

CHAPTER

Discover The Secret Foundation
Of Writing That Will
Maximize Your Efficiency
And
Cut Your Writing Time In Half!

n This Chapter—

Background Information

📖 Niche Markets

📖 Target Markets

📖 Customer vs. Client

📖 Features vs. Benefits

📖 Selling Propositions

📖 Your Niche Market

Target Market Analysis

📖 Know Thy Competition

📖 Generate Your List of Key Words

📖 How To Ensure Your Book Will Sell

📖 The Target Market Analysis-Ordered Steps

   ✎ Profit Potential for a Month

   ✎ Guidelines When Doing Your Keyword Search*

   ✎ Purchase Your Domain Name

   ✎ How To Differentiate Yourself

Additional Support

📖 38 Ways to Find a Hungry Market

📖 Survey Your Target Market

📖 Writing Exercises

Special Bonus...Download the *eBook Authoring JOURNAL To Success* ($27 Value) from the following URL...

(FREE BONUS $27 Value)
http://AuthorAndGrowRich.com/bonuses

Background Information

Your target market is the group of people or businesses whose problems you will solve.

Niche Market

Successful entrepreneurs and authors recognize the importance of targeting a **niche market** over targeting the general population. Even with a book "everyone will want" it is still imperative that you target different sub-groups of the general population if you wish to have them purchase your book, your product or your service.

It's been said that **you get rich in a niche** and you go broke when you market to all the folk. So niche marketing is the key.

Your niche market has a "face". Members of your target market must be explored, analyzed and described in great detail in order for you to reach them. These people have problems that you can solve. They are waiting for you to present yourself as the expert who provides solutions to their problems.

Target Market

You must take the time to describe the people who are part of your target market. And remember, they are people with faces, values, and needs. You must get to know them. You must use members of your target market to help you prepare your book, your product and/or your service. The target audience is a rich source of information. Never assume you know what they want, need or would like you to give them. Ask them.

What do you need to know about members of your target market?

- In what field of work will you find them?

- Are they predominantly novice, intermediate or masters in their interest?

- Through what form of media are they most likely to be reached?

- What income level would be a reasonable assumption to make?

- What formal education or training are they likely to have?

- What magazines do they read?

- What are the organizations to which they would belong?

- Is their interest or job a static one or an ever changing one?

- How likely are they to seek help with their problems and where would they likely seek that help?

- What are the problems faced by this target market that I can address?

Client vs. Customer

A **customer** is a person (or business) who purchases a product or service **one time** from an entrepreneur. The relationship is short term. Or in the case of an author who has written several books on the same topic the customer may purchase several books. The definition assumes that the only contact with the author is through the book.

A **client** is a person (or business) who has a relationship with the entrepreneurial author. This relationship is a long term one. It is built on trust and the belief that a continuing relationship is beneficial to the client. The entrepreneur must continually provide products and services the client wants.

In order for a published entrepreneurial author to convert one's expertise gained by writing a book into a long term relationship with the reader several things must happen.

- Credibility must be established through the book that will have the reader consider building a client relationship with the entrepreneur.

- The entrepreneur must invite the reader to establish a client relationship.

- Additional resources, other than the book, should be made available to the reader demonstrating the author's expertise.

📖 Contact information needs to be made available to the readers.

📖 Interactive correspondence opportunities like surveys, signing up for a free newsletter, podcast and/or vidcast (video podcast), subscribing to an eZine, getting free copies of articles, blogging, web sites, providing additional resources via regular mail, involvement in a free teleseminar or consultation... should be provided.

📖 The author must make every attempt to have the reader voluntarily provide his/her name, email address, telephone number, street address or some other way of making contact. This is only accomplished by offering something in exchange for this information. It is your credibility that will entice the reader to do just that.

📖 Bonuses for continued dialogue must be created, produced and used to build a client relationship.

📖 Consider the ways in which the Internet and books make building this relationship an effective, rewarding and economical experience.

📖 There should be a strong call to action at the end of the author's book to direct them into another product/service.

You Absolutely Must Understand The Difference Between Features And Benefits

You *must* understand the difference between features and benefits. Features are tangible and benefits are intangible. Features describe what a product is or has based on physical/tangible characteristics. On the other hand, benefits are feeling oriented. Remember that the reason that people come to the Internet is because they have wants and desires. The key for you is to market to people's problems. This is the *sole* reason that people come to the Internet.

From the list of benefits that you create, you want to distil down to the very essence which is your key benefit. You do this by playing the "Which Means What?" game with yourself.

Your assignment is to record all the features and benefits that your product will provide to your target audience.

Here are some definitions to explain the difference between features and benefits.

Definitions

Feature = What your product IS or HAS

Advantage = What your product DOES

Benefit = How your product HELPS you

Example:

Let's look at the example of a pen. Let's say you design a new fangled pen using a proprietary ink formula that you have developed.

📖 Feature: Has non-blotching ink

📖 Advantage: Won't leave blotches of ink and hence smudge marks on a page

📖 Benefit: Saves you the frustration of making a mess by smudging blotches of ink. It also saves you the frustration of trying to get your ink to flow properly. Finally, this pen will save you money since you don't have to purchase pens as often.

You are now going to create a Benefits vs. Features comparison for your book.

An Exercise:

List every possible feature and benefit that your product offers your target group. Make sure that includes everyone. The key with successful marketing is to focus on the benefits, especially those that make you different in the market place.

You Must Consider The Following Propositions In Order To Better Market Yourself And Your Book

There is a noted difference between a Unique Sales Position and a Unique Sales Proposition. In essence, business position related to your USP has to do with all the points that make your business different. Your business proposition has to do with a concise statement of what makes your business different and is written so that it really makes your stand out in the crowd.

Okay, let's look at more carefully the difference between your unique business position and your unique business proposition.

USP—Unique Selling Position

- Is what differentiates your product/service from all others

- Is a list of the key benefits that your product or service provides that others do not provide

- Is created after you analyze your key words and have studied who your key competitors are and what makes them different

- Is the one thing about your product and service that makes it unique among your competitors described from a number of viewpoints, but most importantly from your target market's perspective

USP—Unique Selling Proposition

📖 Is clearly written so that anyone can understand it

📖 Is written from your target market's perspective

📖 Is written to demonstrate that your solution fills the gap or the negative perception of how your target market views those who do what you do in the market place

📖 Is an unbelievable believable statement for your target market as it demonstrates clearly to them what no one else can do for them

📖 Is targeted to a "niche" market which specific problems

📖 Is a proposition that fills a void in the market and clearly articulated in a sentence and in your book title.

📖 Is a solution to a problem

📖 Is measurable

📖 Is the statement that tells the customer/client exactly 'what's in it for them'

📖 Is an attention-grabber to leverage an emotional connection with your potential client of the customer

Examples:

📖 Discover How To Write A 100 Page Book In Less Than 12 Hours And Never Face Writer's Block Again. Guaranteed.

📖 Finally A Used Car Warranty with NO Fine Print!

📖 Our Service Department Charges You Nothing Until The Problem Is Fixed-And Stays Fixed! In Fact, If We Can't Fix The Problem We Will Pay You To Use Our Top Competitor.

MSP—Multiple Selling Propositions

A Multiple Selling Proposition:

📖 Is exactly like the Unique Selling Proposition except there are more of them

📖 Reflects the fact that your product/service may offer several unique propositions

📖 Allows for the use of several USP's at the same time or at different times to different niche markets

📖 In each case it draws attention to the emotional side of the client

📖 Allows you to market your product/service in several ways

📖 Covers a number of possible differentiated reasons for continued interest in your product/service

📖 Is built from the USP for your book in all your products and services

UPP—Unique Personal Proposition

Your UPP (Unique Personal Proposition) is your million dollar story. It is one of the key components of the Awakened Unconscious Credibility Marketing System™. You have a million dollar story and it is incredibly important for you to know how to position it to leverage your USP. The key to positioning your UPP is to reveal your target market's problems by telling your story.

📖 It is a unique personal characteristic/trait that makes what you have to say as an author worth listening to—it's your million dollar story.

📖 It gives credibility to what is shared with the reader because of who the author is and what she/he has accomplished.

📖 It is what distinguishes your personal background history from others who want the attention of the niche market.

📖 It demonstrates the wisdom acquired and shared with the reader.

📖 It makes the author a "member" of the targeted niche market.

📖 It exhibits true leadership qualities through the power of your own self reflection, and

📖 It offers "hope" for the prospective client as it shows the person you really understand one's plight.

Example:

Glenn Dietzel had a high paying job as a Vice Principal working his way up the ladder to Director of Education, but he risked it all to set two Internet records using the power of Entrepreneurial Authoring. Within 127 days, he replaced his income as a Vice Principal and his wife's income as an Occupational Therapist without any joint venture partners and beginning from scratch.

Within three months of going full time, Glenn made his first $100G on the Internet with a list of fewer than 500 people and an incomplete manuscript launched as a 22-page digital book...again another Internet record.

Your Niche Market Described
The Dirty Dozen—12 Questions
That Must Be Answered

Question # 1
Who is your target market?

Question # 2
Why are they your target market?

Question # 3
What do they want? (Make a list)

Question # 4
Where can you reach them? Where do they "hang out"?

Question # 5
What are their problems? (Be specific)

Question # 6
What can you offer them? What are the benefits for them?

Question # 7
Why should they care about your book? Why should they listen to you?

Question # 8
Why should they purchase what you have to offer?

Question # 9
What is your USP (Unique Selling Proposition)?

How is what you are offering uniquely distinguishable from anything anyone else offers on the topic?

15. Examine columnist topics in newspapers and magazines.

16. Go to the bookstore and check out the shelf space given to the books that are selling. Go to different sections in nonfiction and see how many books in different subjects are placed facing out so you can see the entire cover and get an idea of what is currently hot.

17. Amazon.com—top 20 books are listed.

18. Amazon.com and use the search tool. (Books Tab >Advanced Search> Power Search).

19. USA Today...Every Thursday, the top 50 books are listed.

20. http://www.DMnews.com Get the free subscription of Hardline Copy...new mailing lists available.

21. Visit Yahoo Stores and see what are the hottest selling items.

22. Go to ClickBank Market Place (http://www.ClickBank.com).

23 .Associate Programs...look particularly at those who are not paying significant affiliate payouts (http://www.AssociatePrograms.com). This is a great opportunity for you to get affiliates for your idea with a higher payout.

24. http://www.TradePub.com offers an extensive variety of free trade publications by industry and geography to qualified professionals. Fill out their form and order all relevant publications.

25. Go to Used Book Stores.

26. Analyze back issues of magazines.

27. Examine where people hang out...blogs, forums, discussion groups, RSS directories and podcasts.

28. Look at the list of benefits on "competitors" websites. Write the questions that go with each of the benefits. Now take the questions and write your own answers (or research them if needed).

29. Run an Ask DataBase Campaign and let your target market answer them for you. Let them know Glenn Dietzel sent you and they will give you a great deal or use the following reference URL...

    http://tinyurl.com/2lxwsy

30. Here are a few sites to examine to see what is going on

    Business Trends...

    a. Cool News of Day-
       http://www.getresponse.com/t/263997/

    b. Seth Godin's Blog-
       http://www.getresponse.com/t/263998/

    c. Tom Peter's Blog-
       http://www.getresponse.com/t/263999/

    d. Springwise Newsletter-
       http://www.getresponse.com/t/264000/

31. Here is a site the media use to stay current with trends...

http://www.news.google.com/press/zeitgeist.html

32. Check media release sites like...
http://www.PRWeb.com and
http://www.BusinessWire.com

33. http://groups.google.com

34. http://catalogues.google.com

35. http://froogle.google.com

36. Watch PBS television and other educational programs to stay on top of trends

37. Information in the public domain (books published before copyright laws were in effect). Everything before 1923 is public domain; 1923 to 1963...must be renewed in the 28th year (85% not renewed). Examine public domain using the following sites...

    a. http://www.Copyright.gov/records
       (US Government for works from 1950-1963)

    b. http://www.Alibris.com (Owned by Google.com) (Use advanced search...specify after 1923 and before 1963)

    c. http://www.firstgov.gov

    d. http://www.Thomson-Thomson.com
       (Pay the small fee to do a copyright search)

How To Check Markets Using Your Target Market's Feedback...How To Let Your Target Market Tell You Exactly What They Want!

Here is a great way to find out exactly what hungry markets want. Create a Google AdWords campaign and then drive people to a website where you ask them their most burning question about a given topic. This will help you to determine what your target market really wants.

A website that we really recommend is the Ask DataBase software created by Alex Mandossian and his team. This is the only search engine that is currently available for analyzing surveys.

You ask people to answer a simple question and use their feedback to create your book and other information products, such as seminars, audio programs, e-courses, special reports and future books. Go to http://tinyurl.com/2lxwsy

Remember to create a vivid, detailed profile of your intended audience. You are selling to real people with real needs. The more you get to know your intended audience—the more you "feel their pain: and provide a solution to the problems that keep them up at night—the better you will be able to relate to them and the better your book will sell.

Here's a technique that sales copywriters often use. If you can think of one (or several people) who have the need you're fulfilling or the problem you're solving, imagine that you're talking directly to that individual. Better yet, get feedback from him/her. Feedback is your friend.

Next, you'll discover some of the many ways you could organize your book. Now that you're thinking "target audience," you're ready to think of how best to present your material.

Frank Gasiorowski, now known as "Mr. 90-Day Goals" did not believe he could write a book. In fact, for 35 years he lived his university professor's message to him..."Frank, you will never be able to write." Even though he began to overcome this dream-stealing message, he thought he had no time to write. Without this system, he would not, but with it, he wrote his book at rest stops along the I-95 corridor in less than 12 hours. Because Frank has a book, he was able to leave his job. Today he has his own radio and television shows and is an internationally renowned speaker and author.

Visit him at http://www.90DayGoals.com.

What are you going to do

in your book to get

the readers compelled to

begin reading and

keep them going to

the end of your book?

Read on...

CHAPTER

Eliminate Your Competition
By Filling Your Book With
What Your Readers Want AND
What They Need!

Organizational And Writing Strategies
Flow

Flow means:

1. move easily and smoothly

2. Continuous movement

F low in writing is the process of making the reader's experience a positive and rewarding experience. In order to accomplish this, YOU as the author must do everything in your power to keep the reader reading the contents in the book.

For non-fiction and entrepreneurial writers in particular, your objective is to solve a person's problem with the material in your book. In order to do that you must provide the incentives, cues, experiences, and transitions that compel the reader to keep reading.

This can be accomplished in a variety of ways. The important point to remember is to think "flow" and to <u>always</u> write your content from the reader's perspective.

There are two types of flow:

- **Aesthetic Flow**—ways and means to keep the reader reading the book

- **Structural Flow**—the formal organization of the contents of the book

Aesthetic Flow

Consider the following as suggested methods of maintaining flow in your book. These are but a few examples.

1. Organizational Flow

- Point form outlines

- Table of Contents (much more about this later)

- Questions and Answers (more ideas later)

- Headings and Sub-headings

- Breaking up of long text passages (e.g. with graphics, pictures, clip art, quotes, text boxes, line section dividers, text borders, summary statement, personal anecdotes)

- Consistent formatting of page content throughout the book

- Using topics, sub-topics, sub-sub-topics

- Following a chronological order of presentation

- Use of white space—not "crowding" the text

2. Progression Flow

- Logical

- Sequential

📖 Step-by-step

📖 Easy to difficult

📖 Novice to expert

📖 Start to finish

3. Graphics Flow

📖 Flow charts

📖 Planning diagrams

📖 Graphic organizers

📖 Examples and samples

📖 Indices

📖 Maps

📖 Schematic diagrams

📖 Structural outlines

📖 Graphs

📖 Charts

📖 Flow sheets

📖 Spreadsheets

4. Writing Flow

📖 Use words with few syllables

📖 Tell stories (especially ones about the author's experiences)

📖 Hook the reader with introductory statements for each chapter

📖 Include summary statements at the end of sections of text

📖 Connect one section to another with transitional paragraphs

📖 Keep the Readabilty Level at the Grade 7-9 level

📖 Use simple sentences

📖 Write in short sentences

📖 Keep paragraphs small (3-6 sentences-not 10+ sentences)

📖 Use active voice

📖 Include checklists

📖 Involve reader using questions, fill in the blanks, sentence completion, surveys, questionnaires, comment sheets...

📖 Create point form summaries and lists to reduce the reading and break up text

📖 Use repetition to help the reader anticipate the organization and be ready for it (e.g. a quote to begin each chapter that summarizes the message)

There are plenty of other ways to maintain the flow of reading in your book. If nothing else, you now have plenty of food for thought.

Structural Flow

The structural flow of a book is the way that the material in the book is organized. Two factors affect the method of organization.

The **first** is the presentation of the contents from the reader's perspective. Your target market (reader) is more important than you. Always remember that. You are not an effective writer if the intended audience doesn't want to read what you have written.

The **second** is the background that you bring to the authoring experience both as an expert on the chosen topic and your own personality. Don't try to be something you aren't. Your book is your story—both personal and professional. You must decide, among the myriad of choices, how best to effectively present the material to your reader. A term we have coined is the author's UPP (Unique Personal Proposition) as mentioned earlier. This is YOUR unique approach, background, experiences, and philosophy that you bring to the topic. Your personal story around your topic carries a great deal of weight in building reader confidence. This helps convert the customer to a client.

Three structural objectives will be addressed in this section of the book.

They are:

📖 Table of Contents (TOC)

📖 The Entrepreneurial Authoring Genealogy Trees™

📖 The Table of Contents: Ways to Organize Your Book

The Table of Contents (TOC) is the very first thing you work on. It's the beginning of your book authoring experience.

The TOC is:

📖 The blueprint

📖 The action plan

📖 The roadmap

📖 The motivation

📖 The foundation

📖 The first step in the authoring journey

📖 The outline

📖 The first concrete manifestation of your book

📖 The lead generator for the book's content

📖 The do-it-yourself manual

You will first divide your book content into chapters. There are many ways to organize your book other than in the common "chapter" format. Perhaps your topic is best handled in sequential steps or Q&A, but here I will use the term "chapters" to illustrate how to organize your thoughts.

Brainstorming

The term brainstorming means you write anything that comes into your head related to the key word or topic you chose for the brainstorming session. Do not reject any idea at this point. You may group the ideas later, but initially the brainstorming session dismisses nothing.

In most situations, you will be brainstorming alone at first. However, you should consider inviting others who understand your topic. Members of your target audience—people who have the problems you are solving with your book—are an excellent choice for brainstorming. They will tell you exactly where their "pain" is and what problems they need you to help them solve. They will offer valuable insights and perspectives. What you are doing is brainstorming the major topics or concepts that should be covered in your book.

The Entrepreneurial Authoring Genealogy Trees™

You will use two Genealogy Trees™ for the organization of your content. The first one, The Entrepreneurial Authoring Genealogy Tree™ (page 137), will focus on the title and chapter content. The second, The Entrepreneurial Authoring Individual Chapter Genealogy Tree™ (page 140), addresses the individual chapter content.

The genealogy trees are visual representations of how your material should "flow" from beginning to end and all the material in between. Armed with this magical outline, you will be able to write anywhere, any time, any place you can find 5-10 minutes. Your doctor's waiting room becomes an opportunity to write when you have the key words and phrases readily available. It's amazing how much you can accomplish even in small amounts of time when you have the words that get the ideas flowing from head and heart to hand. Writing is the doing part of thinking. Words are triggers for ideas, and your ideas flow out of your head onto the paper.

Writing

Start creating your TOC individual chapters by considering some or all of the following idea generators.

📖 UPP—the unique experiences brought to the book by the author

📖 The list of problems generated in Chapter 3—Your Niche Market Described—The Dirty Dozen questions—Question #5—Problems

📖 The list of benefits that the book brings to the reader. Refer to the list of benefits created in Chapter 3—Your Niche Market Described—The Dirty Dozen questions—Question #6—Benefits

📖 The list of Key Words and Phrases you generated in doing your Target Market Analysis

📖 The questions you asked, the problems you faced, and "failures" you, the author, experienced with the same topic. It's important to realize that the author's stories don't all have to be success stories.

📖 The steps, progressions, or phases one has to go through that solve problems for the readers

📖 The attitudes, skills and knowledge required to solve his/her problems.

📖 The concerns and requests of the target market as revealed to the author through surveys, questionnaires, interviews and contact with the audience members.

📖 The perceived or real "gaps" in knowledge presently available to the target market

📖 The brainstormed list of major topics under the title and sub-title or message of your book

The Entrepreneurial Authoring Genealogy Trees™

Let us begin the organization of your book by addressing the <u>Entrepreneurial Authoring Genealogy Trees</u>™. The large triangle at the top center of the page represents the title and sub-title of the book. If you have an idea for a title and/or sub-title for the book put it at the top of a page of blank paper. If you have not yet chosen a title, you can simply put the topic of the book in this triangle.

This tree is a representation of the thinking process you will employ as you develop your chapters. The next smaller triangles represent the chapter titles or topics. So under the umbrella of a book title you now create a list of chapter titles using the sources mentioned above. Reject nothing at this point.

You may find you have enough chapters to consider another book or even a series. That's fine. In that case you will have much of the work already done, and after writing one book you will have a personal template for all others. That will make the work so much easier.

At this organizational stage, you must concentrate only on the chapter topics. You'll start with a set of key concepts to guide your writing.

Take your time here. Nothing is carved in stone, including the title and sub-title. So don't panic. Once you have these done, you will go back to your list of possible chapter topics and do one or more of the following:

- Look at the list of topics for chapters and decide if any of them could be grouped. If so, what would the new topic be? Don't eliminate any of the ideas from this grouping. You will use them in the next step of writing the individual chapter content.

- Look at the topics and determine whether there is a logical and efficient way to list them chronologically. Remember the concept of Flow that was discussed earlier.

- Do the key words for each chapter fit with the overall topic of the book? Does each topic add to—not detract from—the main message?

- Using your best skills, can you now create a chapter title that will draw people into the content? Remember that your Table of Contents (TOC) will likely be used on your sales page to show prospective customers what they will be getting. Each chapter addresses a problem or "pain," so the "pain" should be evident in the title or subtitle. Don't get too fancy here with "poetic licence" titles. Appeal to the emotions of the reader. You can always change your titles later, but the process of thinking through each chapter helps clarify your writing when you get to it.

    Make a list of all your chapter headings under the book title and sub-title so you can see what your working TOC looks like. Put your name, as the author, under the sub-title. You are an author. Start thinking like one.

Even when you get everything transferred to your computer and start writing your book, don't destroy these notes. You will still need all the information you have generated.

Entrepreneurial Authoring Genealogy Tree™

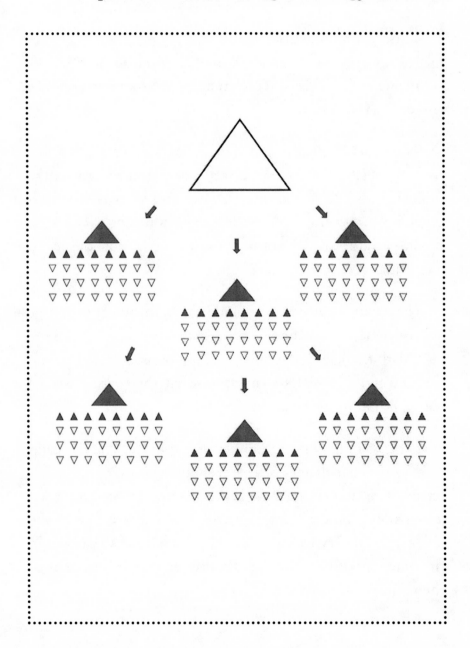

The Entrepreneurial Authoring
Individual Chapter Genealogy Tree™

This Entrepreneurial Authoring Individual Chapter Genealogy Tree™ is a continuation of the previous tree. It, too, is intended to be a visual representation of how to organize the content in your book.

The focus here is on individual chapters. Notice that you have not really begun to write your book. You are still in the brainstorming and planning stages. This step is the most crucial. Once you get the organization done and clarified, it becomes the road map you will use to begin your journey to authoring success.

Place your chapter number and title on the top of your page as represented by the line beside Chapter _____ and the large dark triangle in the middle of the page. If you wish, you can also write a brief statement of what the chapter will be about, if that helps you focus.

Next, you will brainstorm key words that focus on the main ideas under that chapter title. You shouldn't have to start from scratch here. You already have key words from the target market analysis and those generated by the title and message of the chapter itself. Try to create at least 5 sub-topics that would fit under the topic. You can always add, remove or change them later.

The small inverted triangles represent single supporting ideas you wish to address under the sub-topics. They are grouped in threes or triads. Use words and phrases that will act as idea generators so that when you start writing your chapter, you can begin with one sub-topic and have at least 5 supporting points. The sub-topics will become sub-headings in most cases in your finished book, while the supporting points become the text.

Work your way through all of the chapters you plan to write using this same technique before you start writing the book. Remember, you can make any changes you want at any time. As mentioned earlier, you may decide you have two or more books here—and that's fine. In that case record and set aside the ideas for the second book and work on this one.

Once you have completed a Chapter Genealogy Tree™ for each chapter of your manuscript, you now have a very detailed working TOC. You are now ready to sharpen your focus from an entrepreneurial stand point and laser-focus your writing from the perspective of what your target market wants using the principles of Chapter Five. You will then have a strong foundation to complete the 12 Hour Writing Experience as described in Chapter Six.

The Entrepreneurial Authoring
Individual Chapter Genealogy Tree™

Chapter _____

Chapter Writing Tips

Keep accurate records of all information you gather. Being well organized is imperative. And if you are not well organized, hire someone who is or get help so you can continue doing it.

Note: Often you will have flashes of brilliance while you are writing. Record those brilliant ideas in the margins before they get lost. From personal experience I can tell you that it is wise to <u>always</u> carry paper and pen to record those revelations. It's very frustrating to lose a good idea. It's like losing a friend.

With all this data, you are now ready to write. Carry at least one of these detailed chapter outlines with you at all times. You are ready to take advantage of every 15 minute block of time that might suddenly present itself. Thus you can make progress when you least expect it. Make backup copies at all times. Put dates on all revised versions of your writing so you don't waste time looking for the most updated piece of work. This is experience talking. "Last revised June 24, 2008" can be a life saver.

Author your entire book in small segments. Write individual sub-topics. Finish one sub-topic before moving on. Come back to your chapter content after you have finished the entire thing. This will provide you with a better perspective as you begin the first editing process.

It's recommended that you write your entire book from your heart without doing any research. The research that will be required will become readily apparent. There is no need to do more research than necessary. Do take the time to make margin notes about those ideas that will require further reading or research. Highlight them with a marker so you can easily find them later. In fact, color coding your margin notes is a good idea. Then transfer them to a master to do list.

Depending on your personal preference, you may have hand written the chapter content. You must eventually get your manuscript onto your computer.

Run a full spelling and grammar check on one entire chapter. In fact, it may be a good idea to do this with the first chapter you write. This will reveal any problems with your writing that you may not have noticed. Pay attention to the grammar miscues. This will save you time and effort in the future. For example, you may have used too many passive voice sentences or used too high a grade level. You should have only a small percentage of passive voice sentences. And the reading level should be between grades 7 and 9. This is not a university or college paper. You can find out this information by running a full grammar and spell check with Word. A statistical report called the Readability report will appear after the complete spell-check is complete. Use Help in MS Word for more information.

BUT WAIT—just a little longer!

Options For Organizing Your Book

Before you begin writing the actual book, consider the many choices available to organize it. Don't get worried or bogged down; just realize that there is more than one way to accomplish this task.

These organizational options can also be applied to your entire book. For example, the most common one—the Entrepreneurial Authoring Genealogy Tree™—is the chapter method, but there are others. Case studies describe a situation, followed by an analysis to bring out the points you want emphasized. Another option is to provide a story or anecdote and then launch into the content.

The following models are examples of the 30+ choices found in the Entrepreneurial Authoring Mastermind Programs and are only some of the available suggestions. In this program, there are a full range of options, including working with an award winning team for 6 months during your entire authoring adventure. (http://AuthorAndGrowRich.com/bonuses/rich)

- The type of content you are sharing

- Your personal preferences as the author

- The likelihood that your target market readers would respond to one format over another

- The consideration that you probably shouldn't include too many different models in the same book

- The need to have some variety in your material

- The respect for the auditory, visual and kinaesthetic learners in your audience

- The aesthetics of the content on the printed page

- The use of book technology to make links alive in your book if you publish a book electronically

All contribute to the choices you will make among the following suggestions.

OR

Look at it from the question/answer point of view

- What do the end users want or need to know?

- What do you know about the subject?

- What did you need to know when you first dealt with this material?

- What have you learned since using this material or since you created the material?

- How have you seen other works of this type presented? If so, how was it used and how effectively was it used? How could you improve on it?

- What do you have to offer your audience and how best do you share that information?

- What makes your approach to the topic different from other approaches?

Options For Organizing
Your Book—A Brief Description

Remember: Begin with the end in mind. Have the big picture planned before you begin to write and before serious organization takes place. When you start to organize bits and pieces of the material, it will be much easier to put your 'stuff' in piles or folders representing the parts of the final product. You are never locked in to anything, but you must start with a plan. Keep KISS in mind. Keep the reader in mind. Consider whether the reader will access this information in print or from the computer monitor.

Organization of the topic you have chosen can be done in a multitude of ways.

Please remember that your final decision is based on three things primarily—

1. the needs of the reader

2. the nature of the content

3. the comfort level you have with the chosen format(s)

Note: the following suggestions could be used effectively with an entire book, an entire chapter or with only a very small part of the content. For example, RaW Stems™ would work very well if you wanted the reader to actually do something to get them thinking and problem-solving.

Sample Options For Organizing Your Book

Model # 1

TOPICS

Main Topic
📖 Health Care Reform In _____ (your country)

Sub-topics
📖 Who must take responsibility for the reform?

📖 Who is suffering under the present system?

📖 What effect does wait-time have on the public's perception of the present system?

Model # 2

QUESTION AND ANSWER

Supervision of Classroom Teachers

Q: What must be done before a Principal enters the classroom to observe the teacher?

A: A meeting must be scheduled with the teacher and Principal to establish the ground rules for the scheduled visit including: when the visit will take place; what will be observed; which data collecting instruments will be used; where the Principal will sit during the visit; how the follow-up session will be conducted...

Model # 3

RaW STEMS™

Reflecting and Writing Stems are open ended statements designed to get ideas flowing. They are a form of brainstorming. They are based on questions that have been turned around to elicit responses to those questions.

E.g. eBooks have many advantages over print book publishing because with an eBook you can...

These are only 3 examples. There are more than 3 dozen options for organizing your book in the Entrepreneurial Authoring Mentoring Mastermind Program. Whatever format you choose, remember to keep it simple so you don't bog yourself down OR lose your reader.

Now take your crash course in creating powerful headlines that irresistibly hook your reader into devouring your book from cover to cover.

Marjan Glavac was a skilled educator who wanted to make a difference in the lives not only of his students, but children and educators around the world. He self-published his first book, but he (and his wife!) was terribly unhappy with the garage full of books that he had to sell. He used the system you are discovering in this book to launch his second book as an eBook. Because Marjan is an author, today he has created a loyal following of over 60,000 members and is an international speaker and leader in education.

Visit Marjan at http://www.HowToMakeADifference.com.

What is the

single most important thing

you can do as an author to

hook your reader and

keep them hooked?

Read on...

CHAPTER

Discover How To Make
Your Readers Continue To
Swallow The Bait
—Page After Page After Page—
By Writing Great Chapter Titles!

W e all know that the way you say things is often just as important as what things you say. Expert authors know that they must be careful with the words that they choose. Everything that you put before your readers must not just be engaging, but it has to keep their eyeballs glued to the page and their hearts pounding with every idea. You are giving them the secrets to make their dreams come true! Who could stop reading that? Who would WANT to stop reading that??

The format for gluing your readers to your book starts with the title of the book. It should be like the headline of an ad that is pulling in millions of dollars every day.

Next, you need to build great chapter titles. If you see the book title as a headline, consider the chapter titles as the sub-heads. To put it a different way, the headline is the bait that gets the fish to snap, the sub-head is what makes the fish keep chomping so the hook sinks deeper and deeper!

It is imperative that you are able to write titles that pull. A more technical way of looking at it is that your book title and your chapter titles are a series of descriptors that clearly describe your Unique Selling Proposition (your USP). Go back to the benefits list you created when listing benefits and features of your book/product/service.

They're Just TITLES!

Right now you are probably thinking:

"Come on guys! They're just TITLES for Pete's sake! Words can't be THAT important, can they?"

That's a fair question. Let me assure you that the way you word something can mean the difference between success and failure or in our case, between being read and being ignored!

Here is an interesting study...

One marketer discovered the value of words by trying 4 different headlines, marketing a diet product, over a 3-month period. The sales material remained identical.

Only the headline was different in each case (In other words, only the words changed. Look at the huge difference in results.)

The headlines were as follows:

1. Breakthrough New Diet Product!

2. A New Diet Revolution!

3. How A Texas Housewife Lost 23.5 Pounds In 32 Days!

4. Dieting Secrets Of A Desperate Housewife!

The Big Question!!!!

Which one do you predict would outsell all the others and by a wide margin?

I pick # _____ and Why did you pick that one?

The Study Results

Every individual response was carefully tracked and recorded. The actual documented results may surprise you.

Total sales were 165 units over this testing period.

Let me repeat myself.

The ONLY thing that changed in this whole sales process was the headline. Everything else stayed exactly the same!

Here's a breakdown of the results each specific headline produced:

1. **Breakthrough New Diet Product!** 13 Sales (8% of total sales)

2. **A New Diet Revolution!** 8 Sales (5% of total sales)

3. **How A Texas Housewife Lost 23.5 Pounds In 32 Days!** 98 Sales (59% of total sales)

4. **Dieting Secrets Of A Desperate Housewife!** 46 Sales (28% of total sales)

Why do you think that number three out-pulled every other headline by a lot?

I'll tell you. Number three alluded to a REAL STORY. A REAL person who lost REAL WEIGHT in a REAL AMOUNT OF TIME. It combined in a sense the UPP with the USP. The target market that this ad was aimed at could identify with that, and thus they bought the product.

What if the advertiser just crafted headline #1 and wouldn't change it? He would have lost 92% of his sales!!

What a lesson! You need to make sure that you craft a book title and chapter titles that will continually sell your readers on why they need to keep reading AND why they need to buy what you are selling!

Power Action Words

The following is a list of Power Action Words that successful authors use in chapter titles and throughout their chapters to keep their readers nailed to their books:

1. Discover	17. Throttle
2. Eliminate	18. Magnify
3. Build	19. Unravel
4. Reduce	20. Identify
5. Avoid	21. Gain
6. Save	22. Achieve
7. Grow	23. Motivate
8. Generate	24. Listen
9. Compound	25. Improve
10. Benefit	26. Think
11. Solve	27. Change
12. Produce	28. Balance
13. Craft	29. Control
14. Execute	30. Polish
15. Deliver	31. Capture
16. Launch	32. Vary

A <u>bonus tip</u> for you when using these and other Power Action Words is to avoid using an 'ing' at the end of the word. i.e. "Making More Money While Staying At Home." Instead, go with 'Make More Money While You Stay At Home'. It is more powerful and more promising.

Remember, chapter titles are like the subheads for each section of your book. You want each title to be so engaging and to nail the 'hungry button' on your readers so well that they cannot stop reading until they have devoured the whole book! Other important 'headline'-writing tips for your chapter titles follow. Choose three and apply them directly to your book right now!

1. You must tell the truth.

2. You must be believable.

3. You must overcome inertia and sloth.

4. Clarity is more important than vocabulary.

5. Writing "down" will catch the most sales.

6. Everyone is the same. We're all humans.

7. The four questions you must have a 'bang-on' good answer to in your chapter titles are:

    📖 Why should your targeted prospect read and listen to you?

    📖 Why should your targeted prospect believe what you have to say?

📖 Why should your targeted prospect do anything about what you're offering?

📖 Why should your targeted prospect act NOW?

In other words, each title should specifically address and meet a need that your market has.

Some great examples of proven titles that draw readers in include:

1. "Do you make these mistakes in English?"

2. "Would you give 1$ for 16 dancing lessons if—"

3. "The Mystery Of Lovemaking solved"

4. "Get Plump!"

5. "Reduce 33 pounds!"

6. "Here's An Extra $50 Grace—I'm Making Real Money Now"

7. "They laughed..."

8. "To People Who Want To Write..."

9. "$1,000 Help To Be Your Own Boss!"

10. "Self Mastery...The Key To Life's Riches"

11. "1944's SEX Discoveries Now Revealed"

12. "I Like Being With A Man Who Knows What He's Doing!"

13. "They All Laughed When I Said I Was Going To Start My Own Business.

I'll bet for more than a few of these titles, you were trying to imagine what product was being pitched!! That is good news! That means that they work like titles/headlines should!

When you are hunkering down to start thinking of your chapter titles, use the AIDA formula to help you with the building blocks:

A — The title should grab your readers' **ATTENTION** and hold it in a vice-like grip!

I — A great title will be the match to start a fire of **INTEREST** under your reader!

D — Your chapter title should reach into your readers' core and touch on their longings and **DESIRES**.

A — The title that you want will force the reader to stop everything he's doing and plan on how he must take **ACTION**!

Power Action Phrases

Okay, because I am such a great guy ☺, I am going to go ahead and give you a whole wheelbarrow full of Power Action Phrases that you can use in your chapters so that your readers won't stand a chance!

1. Free (the most powerful word)...You (the other most powerful word)...

   Example: You Can Start Building Your Financial Empire Today, With This Free Report!

2. Discover...Announcing...

   Example: Announcing the Latest Discovery in Yogurt Production...and How It Will Improve Your Love Life!

3. Do You...Last Chance...

   Example: Do You Want to Miss Your Last Chance at True Love?

4. Secret Of...Bargains...

   Example: Secret Techniques of Shop-Aholics That Garner Bargains in   Every Store!

5. New Always...Yes...

   Example: Your Clothes Will Look Like New, Always! Yes, Even After Coming Right Out Of The Dryer!

6. Now Is...Love...

   Example: Now Is The Time to Melt Pounds Off, Even If You Love Cheesecake So Much That You Can't Give It Up!

7. Amazing...Hate...

   Amazing new technique builds muscle for people who hate sweating!

8. Facts You Should...How Much...

7. Facts You Should Know About Personal Lubricant. How Much Is Too Much?

9. Breakthrough...How Would...

Breakthrough In Medicine! How Would You Like To Never Be Itchy Again?

10. At Last...This Is...

At Last! No More Bickering Children! This Is What Thousands Of Parents Have Been Waiting For!

11. Advice To...Only Way...

12. The Truth Of...Sale...

13. Protect...Hurry...

14. Life... How To...

15. Here Is The...Suddenly...

16. Introducing...It's Here...

17. Just Arrived... Important Development...

18. Improvement...Sensational...

19. Remarkable...Revolutionary...

20. Startling...Miracle....

21. Offer...Quick...

22. Easy...Wanted...

23. Challenge Advice To...

24. The Truth About...Compare...

25. Bargain...

And now we're going to give you <u>some</u> of our secret stash of headline/chapter title tips that we've collected over the years and <u>still use every day!!</u>

1. Never use all upper case letters. We've found that caps on each word in the headline makes them noticeable.

2. Use "quotation" marks surrounding your headline.

3. You need to aim your appeal at basic human needs:

  📖 Making money

  📖 Saving effort

  📖 Impressing others

  📖 More leisure time

  📖 Self-improvement

  📖 The need to belong

  📖 Security

  📖 Getting something others can't

Author John Caples, in **Advertising For Immediate Sales**, says the following:

"A. First and foremost, try to get your target market's self-interest into every headline you write. Make your headline suggest to reader that here is something he wants. This rule is so fundamental that it would seem obvious. Yet the rule is violated everyday by scores of writers.

B. If you have news, such as a new product, or a new use for an old product, be sure to get that news into your headline in a big way.

C. Avoid headlines that merely provoke curiosity. Curiosity, combined with news or self-interest, is an excellent aid to the pulling power of your headline, but curiosity by itself is seldom enough. This fundamental rule is violated more often than any other. Every issue of every magazine and newspaper contains headlines that attempt to sell the reader through curiosity alone.

D. Avoid, when possible, titles that paint the gloomy or negative sides of the picture. Take the cheerful, positive angle.

E. Try to suggest in your title that here is a quick and easy way for the reader to get something he wants."

Great advice, isn't it? You can see why chapter titles are so incredibly important! Imagine your readers thinking that they can browse through your book, you know, a cursory read! As you watch them, you see how they are suddenly <u>riveted</u> to your book. They are trying to pull themselves away <u>but they can't</u>! They have to keep reading and reading and reading because you have reached in through their eyes and grabbed their heart—where they dream-and you won't let go until they take action. Good for you!

Now, as a special bonus for you, we are giving you a safety net! Yes, a safety net of ONE HUNDRED TRIED-AND-TRUE, NEVER FAIL HEADLINES/CHAPTER TITLES for you to use when you are absolutely, positively <u>stuck</u>! Here they are! Tweak them as you will to meet your immediate needs. (We always loved having an ace up our sleeves when I was struggling to write something!)

1. The Secret Of Making People Like You

   Formula: The Secret Of...

   Example: The Secret Of Discovering Untapped Niches Online

2. A Little Mistake That Cost A Farmer $3,000 A Year

   Formula: A Little Mistake That...

   Example: A Little Mistake That Almost Cost Me My Marriage

3. Advice To Wives Whose Husbands Don't Save Money—By A Wife

   Formula: Advice To...By A...

   Example: Advice To Business Class Travelers-By A Fortune 100 Executive

4. The Child Who Won The Hearts Of All

   Formula: The...Who Won The Hearts Of All

   Example: The Figure Skater Who Won The Hearts Of All

5. Are You Ever Tongue-Tied At A Party
   Formula: Are You Ever...
   Example: Are You Ever Uneasy In Your Banker's Office

6. How A New Discovery Made A Plain Girl Beautiful

7. How To Win Friends And Influence People

8. The Last Two Hours Are The Longest—And Those Are The Hours You Save

9. Who Else Wants A Screen Star Figure?

10. Do You Make These Mistakes In English?

11. Why Some Foods Explode In Your Stomach

12. Hands That Look Lovelier In 24 Hours—Or Your Money Back

13. Why Some People Almost Always Make Money In The Stock Market

14. You Can Laugh At Money Worriers—If You Follow This Simple Plan

15. When Doctors "Feel Rotten", This Is What They Do

16. It Seems Incredible That You Can Offer These Signed Original Etchings—For Only $5 Each

17. Five Familiar Skin Troubles—Which Do You Want—For Only $1 Each

18. Which Of These $2.50 To $5 Money-making books Do You Want—For Only $1 Each

19. Who Ever Heard Of A Woman Losing Weight—And Enjoying 3 Delicious Meals At The Same Time?

20. How I Improved My Memory In One Evening

21. Discover The Fortune That Lies Hidden In Your Salary

22. Doctors Prove Two Out Of Three Women Can Have More Beautiful Skin In 14 Days.

23. How I Made Fortune With A "Fool Idea"

24. How Often Do You Hear Yourself Saying: "No, I Haven't Read It, I've Been Meaning To"

25. Thousands Have This Priceless Gift-But Never Discover It!

26. Those At Fault When Children Disobey?

27. How A 'Fool Stunt' Made Me A Star Salesman

28. Have You These Symptoms Of Nerve Exhaustion?

29. Guaranteed To Go Through Ice, Mud, Or Snow—Or We Pay The Tow!

30. Have You A "Worry" Story?

31. How A New Kid Kind Of Clay Improved My Completion In 30 Minutes

32. 161 New Ways To A Man's Heart—In The Fascinating Book For Cooks

33. Profits That Lie Hidden In Your Farm

34. Is The Life Of A Child Worth $1 To You?

35. Everywhere Woman Are Raving About This Amazing New Shampoo!

36. Do You Do Any Of These Ten Embarrassing Things?

37. Six Types Of Investors—Which Group Are You?

38. How To Take Out Stains...Use (Produce Name) And Follow These Easy Directions

39. Today...Add $10,000 To Your Estate—For The Price Of A New Hat

40. Does Your Child Ever Embarrass You?

41. Is Your Home Picture-Poor?

42. How To Give Your Children Extra Iron—These 3 Delicious Ways

43. To People Who Want To Write—But Can't Get Started

44. This Almost-Magical Lamp Lights Highway Turns Before You Make Them

45. The Crimes We Commit Against Our Stomachs

46. The Man With A 'Grasshopper Mind'

47. They Laughed When I Sat Down At The Piano—But When I Began To Play!

48. Throw Away Your Oars!

49. How To Do Wonders With A Little Land

50. Who Else Wants Lighter Cake—In Half The Mixing Time.

51. Little Leeks That Keep Men Poor

52. Pierced My 303 Nails...Retains Full Air Pressure

53. No More Back-Breaking Garden Chores For Me—Yet Ours Is Now The Show-Place Of The Neighborhood

54. Often A Bridesmaid, Not A Bride

55. How Much Is "Worker Tension" Costing Your Company?

56. To Men Who Want To Quit Work Someday

57. How To Paint Your House To Suit Yourself

58. Buy No Desk-Until You've Seen This Sensation Of The Business Show

59. Call Back These Great Moments At The Opera

60. "I Lost My Bulges And Saved Money Too"

61. Why (Brand Name) Bulbs Give More Light This Year

62. Right And Wrong Farming Methods—And Little Pointers That Will Increase Your Profits

63. New Cake Improver Gets You Compliments Galore!

64. Imagine Me...Holding An Audience Spellbound For 30 Minutes

65. This Is Marie Antoinette—Riding To Her Death

66. Did You Ever See A "Telegram" From Your Heart?

67. Now Any Auto Repair Job Can Be A 'Duck Soup' For You

68. New Shampoo Leaves Hair Smoother—Easier To Manage

69. It's Such A Shame For You Not To Make Good Money—When These Men Do It So Easily

70. You Never Saw Such Letters Such As Harry And I Got About The Pears

71. Thousands Now Play Who Ever They Thought They Could

72. Great New Discovery Kills Kitchen Odors Quick!—Makes Indoor Air "Country-Fresh"

73. Make This 1-Minute Test Of An Amazing New Kind Of Shaving Cream

74. Announcing...The New Edition Of The Encyclopedia That Makes It Fun To Learn Things

75. Again She Orders..."A Chicken Salad, Please"

76. For The Woman Who Is Older Than She Looks

77. Where You Can Go In Such A Good Used Car

78. Check The Kind Of Body You Want

79. "You Kill That Store—Or I'll Run You Out Of The State!"

80. Here's A Quick Way To Break Up A Cold

81. There's Another Woman Waiting For Every Man-And She's Too Smart To Have "Morning Mouth"

82. This Pen "Burps" Before It Drinks—But Never Afterwards!

83. If You Were Given $200,000 To Spend—Isn't This The Kind Of (Type Of Product, But Not Brand Name) You Would Build?

84. "Last Friday...Was I Scared!—My Boss Almost Fired Me!"

85. 76 Reasons Why It Would Have Paid You To Answer Our Ad A Few Months Ago

86. Suppose This Happened On Your Wedding Day!

87. Don't Let Athlete's Foot "Lay You Up"

88. Are They Being Promoted Right Over Your Head?

89. Are We A Nation Of Low-Brows?

90. A Wonderful Two Years' Trip At Full Pay—But Only Men With Imagination Can Take It

91. What Everybody Ought To Know...About This Stock And Bond Business

92. Money Saved—Bargains From America's Oldest Diamond Discount House

93. Former Barber Earns $8,000 In Four Months As A Real Estate Specialist

94. Free Book—Tells You Twelve Secrets Of Better Lawn Care

95. Greatest Gold Mine Of Easy "Things To Make" Ever Crammed Into One Big Book

96. $80,000 In Prizes! Help Us Find The Name For These New Kitchens

97. Now! Own Florida Land This Easy Way...$10 Down And $10 A Month

98. Take Any Of These Three Kitchen Appliances—For $8.95 (Values Up To 15.45)

99. Save Twenty Cents Off Two Cans Of Cranberry Sauce—Limited Offer

100. One Place Setting Free For Every Three You Buy!

Your "Swipe File"

There you have it. One hundred Powerful Chapter Titles that you can peruse, use and abuse! Will they all fit into what you are writing or selling? Absolutely not! What you can do, though, is take the essence of these headlines and change them slightly to fit what you need. And, do you know what? You could easily have your own file of literally thousands of eye-catching, powerful titles and headlines that you could refer to any time you want to.

Set up a file of powerful headlines (remember that chapter titles and headlines are the same in this case). We call ours the Swipe File. Whenever you see a headline that really makes you want to read an ad or sales letter, be sure to clip it or write it down. Review your swipe file whenever you need to write headlines. You may be able to alter a great headline to suit your needs. Or at very least, great work has a way of stimulating your creative juices.

Here is an example how to improvise these time tested headlines.

The "Borrow-A-Proven-Winner" Approach

This technique 'borrows' words, phrases, and formats from famous headlines such as those above. With this method, you take individual components from existing headlines and tweak them to suit your title/chapter titles. You can also choose from different headlines that you like, combine features of several to create a cross-bread. You simply combine together a few parts that you like, and substitute your benefit or offer to suit the title/chapter title.

Never copy someone else's headline word for word, as you want to make sure your book is different from anyone else's. Copying someone else's title is tantamount to theft. But no one can take exclusive ownership of any word or phrase. You're always free to use any word or description in your own unique way.

It's an easy way to put together a solid headline in just minutes. The key is to utilize many of the headlines that resonate well with you and to have instant access to them as you are brainstorming your own titles.

Keep your eyes open for headlines that you like and keep a file of them. You never know when you will want to adapt a phrase or technique from one you like. With your own file of collected headlines, which is commonly referred to as a 'swipe file', you will have a ready resource of ideas.

Following are some examples of simple adaptations from original headlines:

> **Original:** "They Laughed When I Sat Down At The Piano...But When I Started To Play!...(John Caples)
>
> **Adaptation:** "They Laughed When I Sat Down At The Piano. They Stopped When I Picked It Up...(Gold's Gym)

> **Original:** Breakfast Of Champions! (Wheaties cereal)
>
> **Adaptation:** Breakfast of Millionaires. (Barron's financial magazine)

> **Original:** "What Four-Letter Word Do You Use When You Have To Write A Check

For Your High Healthcare Premium?"
(Jerry Fisher)

Adaptation: "What Four-Letter Word Do You Use After Stepping On To The Bathroom Scale?"

Original: "To People Who Want To Write...But Can't Get Started"

Adaptation: "To People Who Want To Own A Beautiful House...But Can't Get Started With A Regular Savings Plan."

Original: "10 Ways To Lose Extra Weight And Keep It Off!"

Adaptation: "3 Ways To Rid You Home Of Pests And Keep Them Away For Good!"

"Never Forget These Very Important Ideas!"

Things to remember (tie a string around your finger for these!)

- A chapter title should have all the subtlety of a hand-grenade. Look, you have only one brief chance to capture your reader's attention. Don't waste it. If you're clever, cute, or vague, you'll probably lose the reader.

- The type of title that draws the reader in focuses on the most relevant benefit your customers get by doing business with you. A powerful, meaningful advantage, clearly stated, will always win you a strong share of qualified prospects.

In closing, remember that writing chapter titles that will draw your readers in—like no other—are not always going to come easily to you, but they are VITALLY IMPORTANT!!

Practice makes perfect—so continue practicing with every chance that you get and you will begin to see the difference. Think like your target market. What do they want? Why should they read this? How can I help them?

With this in mind, it's time to start filling in those chapters. Write on!

AUTHOR & GROW RICH HALL OF FAME

CONGRATULATIONS

Dr. Larry Smith

Glenn Dietzel
Glenn Dietzel

Dr. Larry Smith is not your ordinary chiropractor. Not only does Dr. Larry, as his clients call him, dominate his local market because he used the principles in **Author And Grow Rich,** he is also an insightful healer and Ironman triathlete who has turned a shocking tragedy into an amazing triumph. His inspiring book **Embrace the Journey of Recovery** and his passionate presentations have given hope to thousands of people recovering addiction. It was by following the system laid out for you in this book that Dr. Larry was finally able to find his true voice and share his astonishing story of recovery. Today Dr. Larry is one of the most recognized leaders in Chiropractic without a Ph.D.—all because he is an author.

Visit Larry at http://www.embracingthejourneybook.com.

What do you have to do
to provide the reader with
the attitudes, skills, and
knowledge they need
to solve their problems?

Read on...

CHAPTER

6

The 12 Hour

Writing Experience

ith all of the pre-writing work completed, the actual writing of the book becomes a matter of time management.

Schedule large blocks of time in your planner or on your calendar. Make certain that those people affected by this scheduling are "on board" and will leave you to do your work. Make this time to write a priority and others will do the same.

Never underestimate the power and productivity of the **5 minute writing experience**. In five minutes you can write a tremendous amount of content if you have your outline and trigger words in front of you.

STOP Right Now And Do This

Do a simple exercise to prove to yourself that you can author a successful 100 page book in less than 12 hours of actual writing. Time yourself for 5 minutes of continuous writing without editing. Here's what I want you to do right now. Record the following three words: 1. author; 2. success; and 3. dream.

Remember from Chapter 2 I discussed a fundamental principle that our minds think in questions but create best in statements that give us direction and focus. I showed you the power of turning questions into what we call RaW Stems™.

Now I want you to write from the RaW™ Stem...'Author', 'Success' and 'Dream' are intimately involved in my legacy in the following ways_____. The RaW™ Stem comes from the question, "What does your legacy have to do with the following three words: author, success and dream?"

Okay ready, now write for 5 minutes as fast as you can answering this question from this RaW Stems™. Make sure that once you start you do not stop no matter what. You must think "fill the page" and "write faster" as you are completing this writing exercise. You are not allowed to stop and you must not edit anything. The challenge is to get into the zone and write as fast as you can for 5 minutes.

Don't filter. Don't edit. Don't stop. Don't even think right now. Just write from the heart as fast as you can.

Ready? Set the timer. GO!

STOP Reading.
Do NOT Proceed Further UNTIL.
You Complete The Above Exercise!

How did that feel? Count how many words you wrote in that short time. Didn't you write more than you imagined possible in that short amount of time? I know you did.

Take a look at how much you have written. Look at the quality of the writing. Consider how you felt during the experience regarding the flow of ideas. Were new ideas generated by the experience? If you can manage to write even 15 minutes per day in 5 minute sessions you will have accomplished a great deal.

Carry at least one Individual Chapter Genealogy Tree™ with you at all times. It serves a couple of purposes. You will always be ready to write whenever an opportunity presents itself. Those waits in the doctor or dentist's offices will no longer be a poor use of your time. It is also a reminder that you are an "author" and are indeed "writing a book". This book is important to you.

Your writing "trigger" is your Individual Chapter Genealogy Tree™. Use the words and phrases you have recorded under each chapter sub-heading and begin to write. Stay focused on that small section of the book only. Write without picking up your pen from the paper or your hands from the keyboard.

Allow the ideas to flow and let the content spill out of you. Never go back and correct or re-write or do anything that will interrupt the flow of ideas. You have plenty of time to do that later.

As you write and good ideas come to you use the margin of your paper or a separate pad of paper to record them before you lose them.

Use abbreviations of the common words you might use in your book. For example, you might use "b" for business, "l" for legacy and "tm" for target market. Get the "essence" of what you want to say but do it in a manner that will allow you to accurately interpret what you have written when you return to it for editing or transcribing it to the computer (if notes are handwritten).

In order to make the next writing opportunity as productive as possible, you should take 30–60 seconds at the end of each writing session and make some brief notes or keyword list that will act as a "trigger" for you when you come back to the writing. In other words, take the momentum that you have in the current session and give yourself the kick-start you need in order to sit down and write immediately next time. This will prove extremely beneficial especially if you can master the 5–10–15 minute writing sessions.

Armed with these few suggestions and your background information already done, you are ready to do what you have wanted to do for a long time—WRITE!

Remember to "Write from the heart and edit with the mind". Allow your personal experience and wisdom to appear on the page as you write first without editing so the ideas present themselves. Only after the writing from the heart does the editing with the mind enter the picture. This is hard to do for some people but it must be seen as a legitimate goal. You will move from the manuscript to the final book production in the post-writing experience.

Most of all—enjoy the journey. The writing is by far the best part of the book authoring journey. You will be exhilarated by the experience.

Tips To Authoring
A 6 Chapter, 100 Page Book
In Less Than 12 Hours Of Writing
Consider These Reflective Thoughts About Book Authoring:

📖 Write from the heart; edit with the mind.

📖 Write—Research—Edit

📖 Writing is a one-on-one conversation with yourself.

📖 Writing is the doing part of thinking.

📖 If you can talk to yourself and others, you can write.

📖 Always write (talk) to your audience not to yourself!

44 Bullets For Your Authoring Gun:
Tips From The Pros To Really
Knock 'Em Dead!

Use the following writing tips for each of the Entrepreneurial Authoring Individual Chapter Genealogy Trees™ from page 140 as reminders of what you could, should and might try to enhance the content of your book for the reader. These tips come from experienced book authors who have "been there and done that!"

1. Each chapter title should focus on conveying a key benefit for the reader. As well, each of your major points for each chapter should reflect the supporting evidence that, when combined, reinforce the major benefit for the chapter.

2. Key words in your writing should be nouns and action oriented verbs. Active not passive sentences will lead your reader to do something. Use as many key words as possible in the body of your content.

3. The human mind thinks in terms of questions and answers so begin by stating the three concepts that you want to cover in the form of a question. Reformulate the question into a RaW Stem™ as explained at the beginning of this chapter on page 76. Focus your thinking on writing from only three concepts (as represented by the inverted triangles on the Entrepreneurial Authoring Genealogy Trees™ (pages 137 and 140) for each point you are making. Remember to focus your answer specifically on solving the problem you are addressing.

4. Be aware of technical language and jargon that your target market uses and recognize but don't overdo the use of it. Your target market may not be as sophisticated as you think. Keep it simple.

5. The use of the metaphor is a powerful writing technique. Either use a metaphor that is universally recognized or one that is specific to your target market (which is even better). Do not under any circumstances stretch the metaphor beyond recognition. You will lose credibility.

6. Use the key words or concepts in the first couple of paragraphs of the introduction to your chapter in order to help you focus your direction. It also sets up the reader's expectations. If possible, connect the previous chapter to this one in the first few paragraphs as well.

7. Summarize your chapters using the key words for that chapter. Remind the readers of the key benefit that was the focus for the chapter. The last paragraph of your chapter should lead the reader directly to the next chapter's topic and focus. This can be done with a quote, a

direct statement, a writing exercise, a question, a challenge, a reflective comment, a "what's next" statement...

8. In order to write in a conversational style, picture a member of your target market talking to you about a problem over coffee at Starbucks and you are speaking with her/him about the attitudes, skills and knowledge they will need to meet their needs and solve their problem.

9. Write with your 'heart' and edit with your mind. Write your entire book before you begin the revision and editing process. In most situations you, the author, have experienced what your target market is experiencing. Give yourself the freedom to sit and reflect on those experiences in order to shape the content of your book. This is your "heart-felt" story.

10. Write your entire book without doing research and only do the research that is absolutely necessary to help the reader. Keep track of those areas that will require further research. The readers want "get to the point" information not the research itself.

11. Force yourself to write as quickly as you possibly can for the first 15 minutes of each writing session. You will find you can write for much longer than that or you may find you have to start with only 5 minutes of intensive writing. It is a flow of ideas you are looking for not a finished product. Always write without lifting the pen from the paper for as long as you can.

12. Write from point form notes that "trigger" emotional responses in you and focus the writing on those key words. Record words or phrases, as they come to you from your subconscious, so you won't "lose" them. Your point-form notes will make it easy to get started and keep going.

13. To launch yourself successfully into the next day's writing make sure you have good point-form notes ready. Read ahead so you are well aware of what you will be writing about next. This will allow your subconscious mind to work on finishing the assignments for you and also prevent you from facing writer's block once you start writing again.

14. If you are an inexperienced writer and you want to establish a writing style and format that works for you here is a suggestion. Write one complete chapter. Choose a chapter that may be easier to write than the others or one that you are really excited about writing. Have it edited and proof-read by several people so you can establish early that your writing style is effective. This will establish your preferred personalized style of writing. With this added confidence the rest will be easier.

15. Have everything you will need readily available every time you sit down to write. This may include food and drink. Keep disruptions to a minimum. Enlist the help and support of family, friends and colleagues to give you the time you need to write.

16. Revise before you edit. Revision has to do with the flow and unity of your material; editing involves the technical aspects of writing such as grammar, spelling and syntax. If you enlist the help of others, be very specific with what you want them to look for and comment on.

17. Organize your book logically to make it most useful for your readers. Your TOC and Introduction should make it very clear to the reader the "road map" of your book. Consider where your reader is starting from on this learning journey and where you want this person to be at the end of the journey.

18. A great way to add value to your book is to add worksheets, checklists, flowcharts, timelines, anecdotes, examples, illustrations, success stories and action plans—anything to help readers implement what you've taught them. The more benefit readers get from applying your principles and becoming involved in the process, the more eager they'll be to buy whatever else you're selling.

19. ASK = **A**ttitudes, **S**kills and **K**nowledge. These are the three kinds of information you should be sharing with your readers. The most important of these is attitude. Set a goal of changing the attitude, approach, beliefs, approaches, techniques...of the reader. The skills can be addressed by the things you have the reader do—a quiz, writing assignment, list, brainstorming activity, checklist...that engages the reader in actually doing something. The knowledge is the easiest of the three and although important is less important than the other two. Plan on having all three addressed in every chapter with attitude and skills the main emphasis.

20. Never assume that readers know what you know. When you're an expert, it's easy to assume your readers know things that are perfectly obvious to you. If they don't know what you're talking about, they'll be confused and may feel stupid. I call this common mistake "A therefore C." For example, if you're explaining how to make hot chocolate, you might say "Put the cocoa powder in the cup [A] and enjoy your delicious hot chocolate [C]." What happened to Step B—add boiling water? Now that might seem overly simplistic, but it is a very common error among writers. The best way to avoid this mistake is to have someone else read your manuscript, paying special attention to logical flow and hidden assumptions.

You're just too close to your own material to make this assessment yourself. Providing clear, logical, complete explanations will provide your readers with the greatest value. It is better to have too much information than too little.

21. Provide enough background information to the reader to assure that they can understand what it is you are explaining. You can accomplish this very easily with links to the Internet and items in the Appendix. Don't overburden your reader with too much detail in the text itself.

22. Remember the skill level of your audience—novice, experienced, expert (master). This will affect the writing style you employ, the amount of jargon you use, the background information required, the support materials you need and the additional products/services you offer the reader as follow-up to your book.

23. Pay attention to details to avoid distractions and keep your readers' trust. If you think details don't matter, try calling 912 instead of 911 the next time you need an ambulance. Careless errors in your writing are a distracting roadblock to busy readers who could be doing a million other things besides reading your book. At worst, they have a profound impact on readers' confidence in your authority. If you can't get the little things right, why should they trust you about the big things? Publishing a book that's riddled with typos and other errors also sends a message to readers that you don't care enough to make the effort to get things right—hardly the image an expert wants to convey.

24. A pretentious academic writing style will not endear yourself to your readers. Stiff, formal writing doesn't

work outside academic publications. Writing the way you talk is a much more effective way to communicate. In fact, reading aloud the rough draft of your book rather than reading it silently to yourself can be a fast, easy, powerful way to test that your message is coming across in an effective and conversational style. Or have someone else read your book to you.

25. Write—Revise—Research—Edit is a good formula for success. Write your entire book before revising, editing and proof-reading. Do any research that is necessary—and only what is necessary—in order for the reader to understand what you want them to know. Do the final edit of your draft copy before formatting it and sending it to be e-published and then published in print book format.

26. Writing is a one-on-one conversation that you have with yourself. But a word of caution—don't ever forget who you are writing to and ultimately who you are writing for-your target market. It is your book but it's not written for you. Your book is the solution to your target market's problems.

27. Writing is the doing part of thinking. You should be recording everything that comes into your mind at any time, anywhere you happen to get the idea, and in a manner that ensures your ideas are not lost. Scraps of paper get lost. And so do good ideas. Your subconscious will give you all the help you need to develop the content of your book!

28. Mark on the calendar or day planner large blocks of time for writing. If authoring your book is important (and it should be!) to you then schedule some prime time to do it. What gets scheduled gets done.

29. Tell as many people as possible what you are doing, why you are doing it, what a book is, what your book is about, what you have always dreamed about, how you intend to change your life, what kind of help you need...because there are hundreds of people out there willing to help you fulfill your dream if only they knew about it! Believe me!

30. When and where you write is also important. Pick your time and place. Are you a morning person, afternoon person or evening person or heaven forbid—a 2:00 a.m. in the morning writer?☺ Know your best time to write and schedule writing time accordingly. Choose a location that inspires you.

31. Think 'flow' when you write which means that you must organize your material first then write with purpose. Your purpose, besides solving problems, is to allow the reader to move (flow) through the material in a meaningful, seamless and proficient manner. This is not an accidental journey. Make your chapters flow logically. Introduce each chapter with an overview of what is to be done. And end each chapter in a way that leads the reader to the next chapter.

32. Write thinking "draft" not finished product; refine it later. Your first time through the writing process should come from your head. It's the recording of your knowledge, skills, attitudes—your wisdom! What you have to share with others that is important to them will literally 'flow' out of you onto the pages. What a great place to begin!

33. Write non-stop once you get going. Think about "filling the page" every time you start a new one. This is a great tip to keep you writing and to keep ideas flowing. No going back to correct or perfect! And write as long

as you are "in the flow" if possible. If you must stop or get interrupted record the main ideas you were working on so you can start later without a fresh start. For the first draft, scribble if you wish, but make sure that your handwriting notes are at least legible. It is frustrating and embarrassing if you can't read your own writing. Transcribe your hand-written notes during times of the day when you are at your "least creative". Keyboarding is a no-brainer activity if you already have the notes in front of you. In fact, doing it this way will likely trigger more ideas as you do the transcribing. Use abbreviations—standard or invented ones—to maintain the flow of your writing. For example if you are using the word eBook simply write "e" or "TPYMB" is The Person You Must Become or "l" is legacy...you get the idea. Don't make your creative writing a neat-freak experience. Just do what you have to do to get ideas on paper as fast as they come to you.

34. Record your good ideas in the margins of the paper 'as they come to you' from your sub-conscious so you don't lose them. Get back to writing ASAP. Don't forget to go back to these margin notes and "flush them out" in more detail before you stop writing during the writing session otherwise you may lose the idea. Make a note as to where this idea may be best used.

35. Don't be afraid to reveal your personality. Tell your story. Sharing your personal experiences and insights will ignite your writing faster than a match to a stick of dynamite. Tell your readers about your first hand experiences, reactions and run-ins. These experiences may be good, bad, weird or funny. For the sake of brainstorming, let me elaborate. The "good" could include success stories, tips, techniques or strategies that proved to be effective. The "bad" could be lessons you've learned from your shortcomings, the client from hell, or something you tried that didn't work out. The "weird" could be something that surprised you, or

comments and experiences that were totally unexpected. The "funny" experiences are ones that will make your reader laugh or raise an eyebrow.

36. Stories are interesting. Stories illustrate things that other means don't. Stories give the author personality. Stories allow the reader to identify with a real person. Stories give the author credibility even if the story isn't one of success. Stories break up the text. Good writing reveals something about the author. Your writing must be benefit-driven. This will happen naturally when you allow your personality to shine through.

37. Be a storyteller. Stories are a terrific way to reveal your personality, and bring your message home. If you don't have a story to share, try an analogy, metaphor, word picture or motivational quote. What you are looking for is a hook. You need a way to hook the reader, and keep their attention until the very end.

38. Silence your worst critic! Who? You! Write without being critical or judgmental, and you'll unleash the author within. Don't edit or revise at the early stages. Let the ideas flow. Don't be judgmental or critical about what you're doing. Don't worry about getting it perfect. Write (or type) whatever comes to mind. Later, you can go back to revise and edit. Remember that "free form writing" unleashes the left side of your brain (the creative and artistic side) to express itself. Nothing shuts down the creative process faster than a critic.

39. Never allow a person who you know will cut your book to shreds (figuratively) to read your book as editor or proof-reader. By the same token don't use a person who won't be honest with you. Find people who will give you honest feedback. When seeking feedback about your book make sure that you are very specific

about what it is you want the person to give you feedback on. Without specific instructions of what to look for you will only get very general comments like "I really enjoyed the book." Or "You've done a great job—you must be proud of what you've accomplished!" This kind of feedback is great for the ego but not for the book. Your ego will get the strokes it needs when you help people solve their problems and they recommend your book to others.

40. Be a piggyback writer. Everybody piggybacks. A lot of motivational writers mention Napoleon Hill, but he got his ideas from Emile Coute, and other books dealing with autosuggestion. The secret to writing a good book or article is to use someone else's ideas as a springboard. Build up what has been previously written. Or take a fresh angle, and look at it within a different context. Personalize it!

41. Ask yourself empowering questions. In order to clarify what your book is about and why you are writing it, ask yourself the same questions a news reporter might ask. Then answer them honestly and completely. For example: "Why is this subject so important to me?" "What do I want to write about?" "What information or skills do I have that I could share with others?" "What information do I have that solves a common problem?" "What can I do to resolve it?" "What makes my approach to the problem unique?" "What can the reader expect from me and my book?"

42. Write a 30-second sound bite. Have you ever listened to a commercial that was a 30-second plug for a product or service? This is a technique that you can use with every chapter that you write. Ask yourself, "What am I trying to say, in a nutshell?", or "What am I trying to prove?" In other words, describe the gist of your chapter

in two to four sentences. This will help you establish your objective. You're more likely to accomplish your objectives if they are clearly defined.

43. Consider your book as a whole. Summarize the message of your book in a couple of sentences. Suppose a reporter asked you, "what is your book about?" You should be able to give a 30-second sound bite. The smart thing to do is include your unique selling position within the sound bite. For example, "My book is a seven day plan for personal transformation. It is like Tony Robbin's Personal Power, but it's specifically written for teenagers and utilizes a proprietary system involving hip-hop and the latest in brain wave research."

44. Short is usually better than long. Limit the scope of your book. Focus on exactly what you want to cover, and stay within those parameters. It is better to be concise and to-the-point than longwinded. Delete information and facts not crucial to your story. Your copy will be easier to understand when it is focused and to the point. Tight, focused writing is the best way to engage your readers. If you have too much material for one book acknowledge that and plan on writing a series of books or a book and series of special reports or a white paper or a downloadable MP3 file, or a DVD or...

You're building up momentum now, and you are writing your book. Next, you'll discover how to spark your creativity and leverage the power of your personal story and your uniqueness.

Scott Armstrong is a successful life coach with a full practice and maintains life-long passion for running. Scott's book launched him out of his sales job of 20 years in order to build his passion of coaching. His book demonstrates how goal setting for marathon and for business—and for any aspect of life—are related. His book is Boston Marathon or Bust: A Proven Step-By-Step Program That Helps You Achieve Your Life, Sports, and Business Goals in Record Time.

Visit Scott at http://www.BoulderCoachingAcademy.com.

Are you afraid of
writer's block—afraid
you won't be able to
get started writing
when you sit down to write?

Read on...

CHAPTER

Your Pre-mind Warm-up—

How To Get

Your Brain Warmed-up

To The Creative Experience Of

Authoring And Growing Rich

You CAN Write A Book—Even In 5 Minute Bursts—REALLY!

I want to show you that you can, without a shadow of a doubt, write a lot in just five minutes. There's a trick to it, though. You won't get as much done if you start by staring at a blank screen and wondering what word to type first.

The secret? It's not difficult. In fact, even a child can do it.

One person who took the Entrepreneurial Authoring Mastermind Mentoring Program for 6 months used this secret fast writing tool to author his book while on the road—not while driving, of course, but while on a road trip. He actually wrote his book from the rest stops along the I95 up and down the Eastern US Coast. If Frank can do this, you can do it too!

The secret? Simply this...

Five-Minute (Keyword) Writing Exercise

Before you do the following writing exercise, you should have completed the one in Chapter 6 (Page 183). Do not do the following exercise until you have done this.

Now, it's time to take your writing to the next level. Once again, give yourself 5 minutes, but this time, I want you to choose one of the triads (one group of three small inverted triangles representing one of the ideas you are discussing in one of your chapters) from your Entrepreneurial Authoring Chapter Genealogy Trees™ as your guide. Do this now, while you're on a roll.

Get your timer, paper and pen ready. You have the triad of words or phrases that you are doing to write about. Any triad will do. Remember to refocus your keys from a question into a RaW Stem™. Now...set your timer and start writing as fast as you can. No editing. No filtering. No lifting the pen from the page.

Isn't that amazing? If you can do that, you CAN absolutely author a book, even if you are a busy person and only have short bursts of writing time available.

The Time Of Your Life Exercise

The following exercise is part of the Unconscious Credibility Marketing System™ found in the Entrepreneurial Authoring Mastermind Program and an instrumental part in our Executive Business Acceleration Coaching Program. This exercise will not only get you thinking and writing; it will get you remembering so that you can leverage the power of your life. You will need this to make best use of your unique history as you write your book and build your business. Remember, your story is a tremendous source of power and connection with your audience.

You are going to create a timeline for yourself and fill it with memories and significant events. Here's what you do:

Step 1: Take out a sheet of clean white paper and set it in front of you, landscape style (wide). Draw a line across the page, left to right. This is your timeline. Write the first year you remember something significant on the far left end of the line.

Step 2: Above the timeline, you'll make a chronological list of the "positive" things that have happened to you. Examples would be things like graduating from school, winning an award, getting married, and other major events.

Below the line, you'll write your trials and tribulations—those events that were the hardest for you to deal with in your life. These might include major losses of income, severe illness, the death of a loved one, abuse, divorce, and other tragedies that have had a "negative" impact on you.

Step 3: Keep this timeline somewhere easy for you to find and update. What you'll discover is that once you start thinking about your life in this way, things that happen throughout the day will remind you of things you probably haven't thought of in a long time. Be sure to WRITE these events in your timeline.

Remember, there is often more power in your difficulties and "failures" than in your successes, because your troubles have tempered you. As you share parts of your life with people through the stories you tell in your book, you will forge a bond with your reader. Think about it. Are you more likely to want something that comes from an impersonal source, or one that comes from someone who has a story that you can relate to?

Tap into the power of your life story. Don't be afraid to share your story with others. It will help you build lasting relationships as you grow your business—and your wealth.

Tap Into The Unbelievable Personal Power Of YOUR Unique Story

If you're like most people, you don't think you're special. You think you're just doing the best you can in life. But you're wrong. Dead wrong! You are special. There is nobody on earth exactly like you. And here's what's amazing about your story...

No matter where you live, no matter who you are, no matter what has happened to you in the past—

You have a million dollar story. Yes, you do! You can discover what's unique about you and put that story to work for you. Here's how to get started.

Discover Your Uniqueness In Three Easy Steps

Step 1: Get Ready To Discover Your Uniqueness

📖 Go to the bathroom if you need to.

📖 Turn off your cell phone and email for fifteen minutes.

📖 Get yourself a beverage.

📖 Sit in an uncluttered space.

📖 Sit as comfortably as you can.

📖 Be ready to write.

📖 Don't labor over any idea or question.

📖 Don't get caught up in worrying or thinking. Just read the thought-provokers and questions, and start writing.

📖 Pick up your pen or set your hands on the keyboard. Write everything that comes to mind as fast as you possibly can. You'll have plenty of time later to sort it all out.

Step 2: Respond To These Memory Joggers

📖 I am grateful for...

📖 Something that makes me smile is...

📖 I never expected to enjoy...

📖 My best trait is...

📖 I developed strength I didn't realize I had when...

📖 My life will be complete when...

Step 3: Answer these questions

1. What key events from my life have shaped who I am today?

2. What is one thing I learned that shaped the person I am today?

3. What are my personal strengths?

4. What personal character traits challenge me on a regular basis?

5. What difficulties have I lived through that have made me stronger?

6. What is my greatest, most potent source of personal strength?

7. Based on what I have discovered, what is special about me?

How did you do? If you didn't have an "aha!" moment, you're well on your way to discovering the power of your million dollar story.

Here is something I want you to keep in mind. As you go about your business over the next couple of days, you may have memories or realizations come to you that will give you valuable information about yourself and your dreams. Be sure to—guess what?—

WRITE these memories down, because...

Writing is the doing part of thinking!

As you develop your business, you will need to go much deeper than this, but it is a good start. Now that you have completed this exercise, you have begun the journey to discovering your uniqueness so that you can put it to work for you in your book—and your business.

Another Simple Way To Spark Your Inner Genius

Always carry a pen and pad with you. There are times you'll get hit with an inspiration for one of your chapters, or an overheard fragment of conversation will give you an answer you've been seeking, or you'll finally wrap your brain around something. You WILL definitely want to capture those flashes of brilliance. Don't let them flutter away. When you make this a habit, you'll be amazed how many nuggets of wisdom come to you.

Never use anything as an excuse not to write your book. Life will have its challenges—it always does—but you cannot allow yourself to let anything get in the way of you achieving your dream of authoring a book.

Now that you've got your creative juices flowing, it's time to find out how to add the finishing touches and turn all those chapters into a "real" book—YOUR real book—YOUR Legacy!

Michelle Yozzo Drake began developing her leadership skills when she realized what the strong women of her family had taught her. She took these lessons from the kitchen to the corner office, where she uses them in her high end coaching program. She teaches women to bring their feminine wisdom into every aspect of life. Her book, **From The Kitchen To The Corner Office: Mom's Wisdom On Leadership** empowers women to advance their careers and enhance their leadership skills more than they thought possible.

Visit her website at http://www.MomsMBA.com

What is the single most
important thing you can do
as an author
to hook your reader and
keep them hooked?

Read on...

CHAPTER

The Nuts And Bolts
That'll Make Your Book Look
Like...Well, A Real Book!

T here are two tasks that remain in terms of writing your book after you have completed the 12 hour writing experience and you have your draft copy of the book completed.

These two areas are Research and the writing of the material that will be included on the Additional Pages of your print and electronically published book.

Research

Do only the research that is absolutely essential to maximize the benefits of the content for the reader. Never do the research before you have written the entire book using your personal recall. In this way, you will be talking to your audience not just sharing information. You will be telling your story!!

Use the Internet as a source of up-to-date information that readers can utilize to give them additional background information or to have current data or to view pictures—diagrams—charts...which would be impossible to put directly into your book.

Extensive research and annotated references should be minimized in the content of your book. Summarize and conceptualize any necessary background information for the reader. Don't bog down the reader with details when the "essence" of what is needed can be summarized in a sentence or two. You may wish to reference information in the Appendix or through Internet links and other resources such as books, organizations, etc.

The most effective way to reach your reader is to "Write from the heart." and "Edit with the mind". Write your entire draft copy of your book using what you already know. Talk to the reader in conversational language. Solve the problem with a minimum of theory and a maximum of practicality. Use the wisdom you have accumulated to tell your story and solve the problem.

Only after completing the entire original draft of the book should you consider what areas may need research. Keep accurate notes and sources for your research. Share only what is needed. Your readers will appreciate it.

Take into consideration the ability level of your target market—novice, intermediate, expert. Consider as well the amount of basic information that absolutely MUST be included in your book in order for the reader to understand what you have to offer.

The Additional Pages

Consider the many sections or pages of a book that are not directly linked to the Table of Contents but contain information you wish to share with the reader. Beyond the nuts and bolts content you should consider adding some or all of the following suggested pages.

Cover Page

You may want to include a cover page if you are preparing your book for electronic publishing. On this page you have the title and sub-title of your book, the author's name, and possibly the copyright date. Other information could be added. In addition there should be a graphic or at least the title and sub-title in fonts that will attract attention. The color scheme for the book should be obvious on the cover page. It is sometimes useful to have a graphic of a book cover for your book also on this page. It is a visual reminder that this is a book.

Title Page

Often the Cover Page and Title Page are combined. If you choose to produce a Cover Page with a minimum of information but a great graphic, you may choose to add a Title Page to your book. This page would then include the basic information mentioned above, possibly some contact information or information about the company/business associated with the book.

Copyright And Legal Page

There are many ways this page can be set up. Take a look at the wording found in several books you already own or that can be found on the Internet. Adjust and adapt the content to suit your own book. In most cases there will be the obvious copyright symbol and year, the person or business to whom the copyright belongs, the ISBN number if there is one, the statement(s) that prohibit the unauthorized use of this material in any form without written permission from the author, a way to contact the author should permission be requested to use the material, and anything else that suits your material. In some situations it may contain an acknowledgment of permission to use certain content from a third party. The basic copyright legislation protects your property as soon as you have written it or recorded the concept. One simple technique to protect yourself and be able to prove the book is yours is to make a copy of the draft form and/or final form of the book, put it in an envelope and mail it to yourself. When it arrives by mail do not open it. The postal stamp with the date on it will be sufficient proof of the date of copyrighting should anyone question it. Let a judge or lawyer open it if needed to prove ownership of the material.

Foreword

A Foreword is basically an explanation about what the book is all about and what you can expect to find in it. Forewords can be written by the author him/herself or by someone else. If you are having someone else write it, make sure that this person would be seen by the reader as a "credible" person to write a foreword about a book on this subject. Give directions to the writer of the foreword so you, as the author, get the maximum benefit out of it. The Foreword should set the reader up for the learning experience and make them eager to read the book. Please note the proper spelling of the word foreword. This is the most misspelled word of the English language according to Dan Poynter.

Table Of Contents (TOC)

Write your TOC in draft form as you are going through the writing and planning process. Include all major sub-headings or sub-topics for each chapter. Make it easy for your reader to see what is in the book. You will also be able to use the TOC in your sales copy to show what is in the book, so make sure it conveys not only what is in it but how you have thoughtfully and effectively organized the information with the reader and her/his problem in mind. With books, authors often don't include page numbers beside the chapter titles or topics, because when you are ready to e-publish (which is your first option with Entrepreneurial Authoring), bookmarks are used in Adobe Acrobat to allow readers to navigate around the book and in some situations the author has each chapter title linked to the page by simply clicking on it. You can do both—have the page numbers and the links. Don't put in the page numbers until all changes have been made and the final draft is ready for e-publishing.

Dedication Page

The Dedication Page is an option that many authors like to use. It is their way of acknowledging the fact that it took a team to help them write the book. This page is sometimes incorporated into other pages like a Title Page if there is room for it. Or it can be a separate page. You can acknowledge anyone on this page who inspired you, provided technical assistance, helped you with editing and proof-reading, assisted you with research, provided moral support...It is an effective way of rewarding your mastermind support team.

Appendix

The Appendix is a repository for all those sources of information that, if placed in the book itself, would make the reader's experience less enjoyable and possibly interrupt the flow of the book. This is a good location for forms and surveys, articles, resources lists, data, et cetera. If you do use an appendix in an eBook, it is advisable to put a hyperlink in the main text of the chapter which allows the reader to simply click on the link (indicated by being in blue and underlined) that will take them to the document in the appendix and then allows the reader to come directly back to the same page.

Resources

Unlike textbooks that often have pages and pages of resources listed it is unusual to have this in an eBook. One of the reasons is that most books are written in friendly letter style not formal academia style. And most authors of books write from their experiences rather than from research. That is not to say you shouldn't or couldn't have a list of resources but the list would be rather short and in most cases listed as an Internet link if at all possible. In this way you reduce the number of pages of information but still provide the reader with the information they may need.

Contact Page

The Contact Page and Further Education Page can be combined. A contact page can be included at the beginning and definitely at the end of your book. This page allows the reader to identify with you as a real person and gives them information so they may contact you if they wish. Placing an address, telephone number, business address, company name, list of contact people, toll free numbers, fax number, email address... on this page makes you a "real" person who has an interest in getting to know your readers. Provide enough information for the reader to contact you in whichever way you wish and enough about you and/or your business to inspire confidence.

Further Education Pages

Remember, you're not just writing a single book and sending it off. You're using the book as an introduction to your business. It's your business card that will instantly differentiate you from your competitors. You need to have an easy to understand action step that is outlined on your further education (Sales) page. In other words, you have to give the reader of your book a compelling reason to stay in contact with you by providing them opportunities to invest further in other programs and services. You want life time clients not a one time purchaser/customer.

You want to accurately and effectively describe for the readers the benefits of engaging further with a strong call to action. The concept of authoring and growing rich involves sharing information and expertise to establish your credibility. Once you have that credibility, you will earn the trust with your readers to take the action you will compel them to take in your book.

Remember the AIDA approach to selling? You grab the readers' ATTENTION, evoke INTEREST, create DESIRE and call them to ACTION. That's exactly what you do with this sales page. That call to action must be strong enough to make your readers go to your website and take the next step.

You want them to know what you have to offer—courses, workshops, other books, reports, articles, teleseminars, coaching, mentoring, audio classes, CD's, eZine, newsletter, website, MP3 recording, weekend retreats, etc. These can be sprinkled through out your book, but the key is to present one strong call to action at the end of your book.

The book is the "door of opportunity" for the customer to become a client by starting a long-term relationship with the author. Take the opportunity now that they are impressed with what you have to offer and turn them from a customer who purchased one product—the book—into a client who will purchase many products and services.

Think of it like a funnel. Here's a hypothetical example for you. Your reader has started with your book. Expand from there to your audio program or workbook. Expand that to your electronic course, your workshop, your intensive retreat, then your coaching program. I'm sure you get the idea.

You don't need to have everything lined up right away, but you must have something to offer. Don't let the end of the book be the end of the relationship with your new client. The end of your book is, in reality, just the beginning. Give your reader a simple but specific action to take. Make your reader desire that next step AND act on it.

When you enroll in the Entrepreneurial Authoring Mastermind Mentoring Program, you will be guided through the process of using the AIDA principle with our Unconscious Credibility Marketing System™ and developing your product funnel through our own proprietary process.

About The Author/Company Page

Personal information about you, the author, and your business is very important to establish credibility. It is also a part of your story—your UPP as it were. Include a picture if at all possible as this again helps the reader identify with you as a real person. Make sure the reader knows what is it that makes you qualified to write this book. And why it is so important for the reader to have the information provided by you. Keep the writing style friendly in tone. Avoid a long list of accomplishments, especially if they are unrelated to your topic. Definitely include endorsements and testimonials that have been attributed to you or descriptions by others as to your expertise.

Endorsements

The use of Endorsements about you as an expert in your field or about the book itself is very powerful. You may use some of them in the content itself, in the About The Author/Company page and at the beginning of your book. And don't forget to use your strongest ones on the back cover of your book.

Testimonials

As powerful as endorsements are from noted experts in your field, there is simply nothing more powerful than testimonials of 'everyday people' who are your target market and who have benefited in very specific ways from your material. Make sure when getting these testimonials you follow the following key principles when going after testimonials:

1. Use the before and after approach that television shows such as "body makeover" competitions use. It is important that your target market sees and most importantly feels how you benefited this person.

2. Have each person tell his/her story. Remember, people remember stories. Coach each person who will be giving you a testimonial how to give one that brings

out his/her story. To get the best testimonials you should coach all persons and don't assume they know what to do.

3. Get audio and especially video testimonials. You will be able to leverage everything you do with the most powerful system aimed at building your credibility, The Unconscious Credibility Marketing System™ with the use of video. Make sure you read the next session and take action on this...From Idea To Leads In <u>ONLY</u> 23 minutes.

From Idea To Leads In ONLY 23 Minutes

We have created a system that will allow anyone—yes that includes you—to dominate your market with video. One of the fundamental principles with respect to marketing your book is the notion that it is not the idea that is valuable, but the presentation of the idea that is most important. In other words, it is not your book idea that is most important but the experience that encompasses your book. The Unconscious Credibility Marketing System™ teaches you to find your million dollar story and position it in your book and in the copy that you write to sell your book. This system also teaches you how to use video so easily and cheaply to begin driving traffic to your website to sell your book, even before you sell it. Find out all the details by going to the following URL NOW...

http://AuthorAndGrowRich.com/bonuses/video_secrets

Summary

One major advantage of publishing your manuscript as an eBook first is that you can include as much information as you wish and leave it up to the reader/client to choose what is most useful. The reader has expectations of being offered some additional products and services to help solve other problems he/she is experiencing and not covered in your book. Ideally, if you are using your book to build your business, and it is my recommendation you should definitely think this way, it is really a lost leader, invitation, business card, lead generator for other products and services. A book is seldom an end in itself.

However, the biggest reason for electronically publishing at first is to tap into the power of the Unconscious Credibility Marketing System™ immediately. With an incomplete manuscript you can have your target market tell you exactly what they want and use this feedback to perfect your book and ensure maximum profitability as you build out your programs and services.

Keep the process simple and uncluttered. You not only can, but SHOULD incorporate the work of others in your book. With a twist, of course. I'm not suggesting you plagiarize, but you can take the best of the best that you know and give it your own special flair.

One of the best sources of information that you may wish to include in your book is what you learn from reading other books. Find out what appeals to you in other books and incorporate this into your book. Imitation is the highest form of flattery, you know! You can learn much from others. You aren't reinventing the wheel, simply redesigning it to suit yourself.

Now that you've assembled your book, it's time to consider your choices for getting the book into people's hands and making MONEY with it!

Ronda Del Boccio knew she loved to write but had no idea how to break out of the "poor writer" mode until she found the step-by-step approach in this book. She co-authored *I'll Push, You Steer: The Definitive Guide to Stumbling Through Life with Blinders On*, which went from idea to best seller in less than six months and created a system called The Storyation Process™. Her next book, *The Kama Sutra of Storytelling: Positioning, Power and Profit* is well on its way. Ronda also happens to be legally blind, but she does not let this stop her doing anything she sets her mind to accomplishing. She says, "If a mostly blind woman can do this, so can YOU."

Visit Ronda at http://www.Storyation.com.

How to access a
Global Market 24/7
with your book...right now!

Read on...

CHAPTER

How To Choose
The Right Platform To
'Unleash The Beast'
And Start Making Money!

Publishing Options For Entrepreneurial Authors

T here are five legitimate publishing options for authors. Before you decide which method(s) you are going to use, educate yourself so you can make a well-informed, wise choice. You don't want to invest thousands of hours into a method that won't bring you the results you want. I've known too many people whose dreams were shattered because they lost the rights to their own work. As an entrepreneurial author, it is my professional recommendation that you never give up the rights to your book. It is your lead generator. It is the essence of your business. It showcases your million dollar story to your target market.

Do you know any authors? If so, ask them about their publishing experience. What was good? What was bad? What did they learn? Listen carefully and watch their body language as they discuss their personal experience.

The Electronic Book (eBook) is a good place to start for any author. You'll discover specifically why shortly, but for now, think of it as a way to start making money with your book right away.

Consider The Five Options:

ePublishing (electronic book)

POD (Print-On-Demand) Publishing (print book)

Vanity Publishing or Self-Publishing (print book)

Traditional Publishing (print book)

Entrepreneurial Publishing (print book)

The PRO And CON Arguments

Consider the following PRO and CON arguments for each of the publishing options. Choose wisely.

Electronic Publishing (eBook)

Before I give you the pros and cons, let me reiterate that we recommend you e-publish before you have your book printed on paper through whatever means you choose. If you're not sure why, you'll understand why in the Pro section that follows.

PRO

1. Has the book "out there" quickly...even with an incomplete manuscript you can start making money.

2. Has a 90-95% profit margin with complete control by the author Because you are not paying for someone else to produce your book.

3. The book is delivered instantly and is always current.

CON

1. Won't likely get you on the New York Times best-seller list.

2. Lose people who want a hard copy book or don't frequent the Internet.

POD (Print-On-Demand) (Print Book)

PRO

1. No inventory of books is required as you print only the number of books you need.

2. To produce a hard cover or soft cover version of your book this is the easiest and most profitable method.

3. Works very well with book sales as you can maintain control of the system without a great deal of work. Delivery systems are automated.

4. Companies like Lightning Source and Lulu are POD companies. This means that when someone orders your book, it is printed, bound and shipped within 1-3 days.

CON

1. Profit margins are less than eBooks because there are costs for the printing etc.

2. An agreement must be reached with a company to supply both the printing and the delivery of the books. Sometimes this will be done by the same company, other times not.

Self-Publishing (Print Book)

PRO

1. As with POD books, you are able to provide the reader with a "real book" with a cover. Reader can handle it and you can autograph it.

2. In most cases, author maintains complete control of the process.

3. Allows you to get a hard copy book without spending time, money and effort trying to convince a Publisher that your book is worthy of publishing.

4. Any book will be accepted and printed exactly as it is given to the publisher.

CON

1. The author will generally make only about 20% to 35% of the retail price after doing all the work.

2. The author invests a large amount of money in copies of the book and is solely responsible for selling them as well as storing and delivering them.

3. To get more copies will require a great deal of time and money to get the book republished and/or revised and published.

4. These publishers are commonly referred to as Vanity Publishers which is used as a slur in the Traditional Publishing industry. It is harder to create author credibility in many cases with a "vanity" published book.

5. Many companies do not distribute to places like Amazon and through the larger distributors like Ingram, so people who do not order directly from the author will not be able to order the book.

6. There is no quality control. If you turn in a book full of errors, that is exactly what the publisher will print.

Traditional Publishing (Print Book)

PRO

1. This publishing method will <u>possibly</u> get you on the New York Times money-making books list; however, your chances are minimal without you actively pursuing a focused marketing strategy.

2. Will garner the most respect from readers who see the book store or library as the primary source of books.

3. By virtue of the fact that you have a traditionally published book, you will have an easier time getting media attention and increasing your speaking fees significantly.

CON

1. The author loses rights to the book for the duration of the contract. The publisher owns the rights to your hard-earned work.

2. The traditional publishing model is probably one of the worst business models, a relic of 19th Century process. The chances of making money are not good, and since the books are on consignment in bookstores, any unsold books are billed back to the publisher and ultimately to you the author.

3. The author loses almost total control of the book's content, cover design...Publishers are investing the money and therefore call the shots so the author will receive little profit on each book in the neighbourhood of 3% to 8%. If the author hires an agent, the profit margins are even less, because the agent's fee is 10-15% of the author's meagre share of the profit.

4. The author has to create a formal book proposal which will take weeks of work, then a tedious and long process of submitting it to publishers. According to David Hancock, CEO of Morgan James Publishing, it takes the average person 100 formal book proposal submissions only to get a publisher to say 'no'. With an agent, the number is decreased by half, if you can secure an agent and agree on a commission structure.

Author Terry Burns interviewed over 600 multi-published authors and found that it took them an average of 6 years to see their first book in print after its 'completion'. He also found that 87% of the authors he interviewed got their first book published BEFORE they got an agent. These authors decided they preferred not to share their hard-won profits.

Entrepreneurial Publishing (Print Book)

PRO

1. Author retains rights to book with higher royalties of 20%.

2. Access to same distribution channels (such as Amazon and Ingram) as the traditional publishing model.

3. Because the emphasis is on building a business around the book and on sales and marketing, the author establishes a high degree of credibility with readers.

4. Also because of the emphasis on building a strong business around the book, the author establishes greater credibility with the media.

5. Due to the unique model of writing the book first and then writing it, there are a wealth of other opportunities that the author can take advantage of (teleseminars, coaching etc.). Refer to the CD that came with this book for more details on "How To Go Deep On Your Book/Business Idea."

CON

1. Authors have to make an investment to get their books published.

2. Book might not be accepted by the publisher.

3. You must spend time to have a business plan built around it to even to be considered.

4. Since your success is the publisher's success, you must also have an understanding of how to build a business for the manuscript to be accepted.

5. The work needed to find a publisher who will take a chance on you and your book may better be spent making money and building a business at least initially.

6. The author is still ultimately required to do the marketing of the book even with the smaller profit margins, although the author may possibly have received money "up front" in the form of an advance.

Rubber Meets The Road Reality Of Why You Need To Consider A New Publishing Model For Your Book

Former Model

Book—(POD or Self-Publishing or Traditional Publishing)

to

New Model—Entrepreneurial book→ Entrepreneurial Publishing

Rationale

Electronic and POD publishing options are great entry level methods because they:

📖 are inexpensive to produce and deliver;

📖 allow the author to maintain control over the entire process;

📖 don't require an inventory to be kept by the author;

📖 can be easily used simultaneously;

📖 use digital technology that allows maximum flexibility in terms of content;

📖 have a high profit margin for the author;

📖 reach the intended audience if the business is Internet related;

📖 are easier to update and republish;

📖 can be ready for the consumer quickly;

📖 use a friendly letter style of writing;

📖 can be readily used at speaking engagements;

📖 put the purchase price of the book in the author's hands before delivery;

📖 prove to publishing companies that you can write and you have a market; and

📖 allow the maximum use of technology with minimal costs (book).

Self-Publishing can be a transitional step between digital and POD or traditional print publishing. The major draw-back to self-publishing is the amount of money invested in inventory with the pressure to sell it or lose money. There are countless stories of people trying to sell a garage-full of books they self-published.

Self-Publishing And Traditional Publishing:

📖 require a great deal of money to produce the copies;

📖 have a lower profit margin for the author;

📖 require an inventory—a large number of books that must be sold;

📖 allow someone else to take control of the book (if a publisher is used);

📖 still may require an electronic version (book) to reach the target market;

📖 require a standardized format for the content;

📖 have a short shelf life of about 6 months to "make it" (with traditional publisher);

📖 Additionally, books that have made it through the process of being bounced around, rejected and finally accepted for traditional publishing face some challenges that many authors fail to consider:

📖 will not hit the shelves in every bookstore around the country;

📖 are not promoted by the publishing house;

📖 will not bring instant fame;

📖 the 6-figure advance is a thing of the past unless you are already a sensation;

📖 fabled multi-city book tour rarely happens, and if it does, it's not all it's cracked up to be;

📖 no guarantee of appearances on prestigious talk shows just because you have a book;

📖 contracts may bind author to a right of first refusal on all future works unless author has legal advice when negotiating it; and

📖 publishers are now including within contracts that

not only do they hold all rights to all forms of media expression of an author's manuscript but also any form of media not yet invented!

All Five Options:

📖 Give the author credibility and expertise in the subject;

📖 Allow the author to build a business around the book;

📖 Produce a book that is attractive and does the job if well written;

📖 Are options for all entrepreneurial authors;

📖 Start with the basic text that is well written and well organized; and

📖 Can easily grow out of a book.

Conclusion

For the beginning entrepreneurial author who wishes to get started making money and building a business, the electronic book is the right place to start.

An eBook gives the author the credibility and expertise in the mind of the potential client quicker, easier, less expensively, with less work, still leaving all the other publishing options as potential future ventures.

With technology to produce, market, and deliver the eBook put on "automatic" producing residual income, it leaves plenty of time for you to build a business and produce additional products and services to expand the influence of the book and grow a thriving business.

The experience of creating a book will lay the ground work for any other writing. It will give the author the "mind set" of the expert, build confidence in oneself, clarify the message for the reader, teach one about building a client relationship with the reader, put money in the entrepreneur's pocket, and launch a business built around a book.

The entrepreneurial model of authoring and publishing is a very new concept in the industry. Entrepreneurial authoring is based on two concepts. The first is the introduction and world-wide acceptance of the eBook as a legitimate source of information. It was born on the technology of the Internet and web designing combined with the acceptance of the "friendly letter" non-academic style of writing as a legitimate method of communication.

The second is the instant access to a New York Publisher because of the pre-marketing that has already been accomplished with your finished manuscript. Instant access to a publisher means you will forego the average 6 year wait to get a publisher to notice you.

The eBook is here to stay, especially since all Generation Xers now expect that reading material is in digital format so that they can read it on their computers and eBook reading devices. Although it may be considered an entry level publishing method it is a huge financial boon to entrepreneurs both on the Internet and in the regular business world with profit margins exceeding 90%.

Entrepreneurial publishing is a logical extension of book publishing. For authors whose purpose for writing a book is to gain credibility as an expert by publishing a book, the concept of moving from book to entrepreneurial publishing is a logical step. This new field will provide entrepreneurial authors with experts in publishing who also understand what it takes to build a business around your book. Entrepreneurially published books will be no different than any other print book except that its purpose will be to build a successful business providing products and services built on the reputation of the author.

The entrepreneurial publisher works WITH the author not FOR the author. It is imperative in a book published for entrepreneurial purposes that information not normally found in "best-sellers" be included about the author, one's company or business, and the products/services offered. The marketing of such entrepreneurial books will also be different from a traditionally published book. In this model, authors will retain all rights to the book. The publisher is there to support the author and one's business plan.

Using the information in this book, you now have the foundation for making money before your book is complete, establishing yourself as an expert problem solver, building wealth, and writing your 100 page book in less than 12 hours of actual writing time using the *Author And Grow Rich* Model.

But if you want to take it to the next level and be guaranteed instant access with our New York Publisher, you owe it to yourself and your dream to become a member of the Entrepreneurial Authoring Program which consists of the Mastermind Program or the Home Study Course. When you take this course, my team and I will take you by the hand and guide you through the entire process so that you cannot help but succeed.

You have a powerful story to tell that will help thousands and thousands of people around the world solve their problems and improve their lives. Don't let your dream of authoring wither and die. Go now to the following URL and get more information. Watch and listen to some of the thousands whose lives have been transformed by the power of this system. It is truly the most powerful personal and professional transformational program that exists today. It begins with you and YOUR book!

http://AuthorAndGrowRich.com/bonuses/rich and we'll help you get that book out of your mind and into the world through our New York Publisher

Next, you'll find out how to get your book in the hands of a New York Publisher without writing a tedious proposal package or enlisting an agent. Get ready—Your LEGACY begins with your book and it is indeed an exciting journey!

Margaret Merrill truly adores doing purpose work with clients. She started off as a student of someone else's system, but she realized that she would have more credibility with her own system and her own book. *Live the Life You Love: Discover Your Purpose and Live It With Intention* is only the "business card" for her thriving coaching business and a nonprofit organization that is helping keep the Navaho tradition alive. Her book has paved the way for selling 5 figure coaching packages and accessing millions of dollars of grant money for her 501 (c) 3.

Visit Margaret at http://www.fulfillyourpurpose.com.

So just how do you

write and build

a thriving business

where you can instantly sell

$5G, $10G and $50G

programs simultaneously?

Read on...

CHAPTER

How To Persuasively
Create And Sell
High End Programs
Off A Partial Manuscript
And Gain Instant Access
To A New York Publisher!

ear Author And Grow Rich Friend:

I'm interested in trying a fantastically bold experiment.

As a former Science teacher and someone who could have easily taught your own children, I loved doing experiments. And so did my students!

If you would like a lucrative but highly unusual challenge, you're invited to participate with me now.

For the first time, I am going to share with you the proprietary system I used to set two Internet records in a simple and free format for qualified participants.

To really appreciate what I'm offering, you should know that the ideas I'm going to share with you are the foundation for all of my business success.

I have never shared this before in the manner I am going to reveal to you.

The specifics of my system, when applied, are more powerful and useable than what I have personally taken away from seminars costing me over 50 thousand dollars.

The focused training process I'll use with you is carefully designed to rapidly turn anyone who is ready to take his/her idea into the marketplace into a competent, competitive rainmaker.

What I Will Share With You Is Private, Privileged Knowledge To Build The Essential Skills To Rocket Your Book/Business Success Just As FAST As I Have (Probably faster).

To be honest, it is proprietary and it has never been revealed before.

Why should you be assured of this?

Because this is the system I created to set two Internet records.

I am going to reveal to you for the first time, the 10 specific steps to going deep on your book/business idea immediately...<u>Before your book is even complete!</u>

Imagine discovering a system on how to make money with an incomplete manuscript!

Imagine gaining the ability to build deep on your book idea right away and know how to do what I have done to begin selling $5G, $10G and even $50G programs off your book idea

Imagine discovering the specific (remember, I am a teacher by training and profession) attitudes, skills and knowledge to rocket you into the market place

I know that this is definitely a lot to cover in my fast paced, non-theoretical webinar, *How To Create An Idea Virus For*

Your Rapid Authoring And Business Acceleration (Value $197). But that's just a portion of the <u>practical</u> business knowledge you are going to learn about in this very comprehensive course.

So in addition...

You will have an opportunity to take what you have learned and apply it immediately to gain profits by thinking through for a half hour **one-on-one** authoring/business strategy session with someone who has been described as one of the most dynamic strategic business consultants in today's market place.

Think that's impressive?

The Best Part Of This Program Is That It Will Work For...

Any Book/Business Idea!

Any Market!

Anytime!

Anywhere!

Why? Because the power is in the dynamics of the system.

This is a proprietary system that has literally caused all of my MBA clients to shake their heads in disbelief! **Because it is a system that teaches you all about leverage and rapid business execution!**

Why would I, with open arms "gift" you:

1. A webinar that will show you a strategy that has the possibility to realistically grow your business 5 to 11 times greater every year while positioning you to be the most preeminent expert in your field.

2. A half hour strategy session with my top business consultant.

I have two very good reasons for doing this: One is Personal and one is Business related.

1. I have personally witnessed and been intimately involved in writing marketing reports with a system that has created <u>over 1.2 billion in increased revenue for clients!</u>

   My goal is to exponentially increase my testimonials from hundreds to thousands over the next 12 months. Go right now to the following URL and experience the emotional impact first hand of these real live stories of how my systems have allowed ordinary people like you and me to live a life of abundance and prosperity we all have the right to have. When you go to the URL right now. You will really understand what drives me to do my best to make sure that the people that are ready to experience the level of success they deserve do.

   http://AuthorAndGrowRich.com/bonuses/webinar

2. In order to follow through with constantly and completely dominating my market place, I choose to joint venture with the best in a diverse and select group of industries.

How do I make sure they are the best? Well, the most profound way to be sure I have the quality control I deserve is to educate, guide and mentor my joint venture partners into becoming unparalleled to anyone else in there industry.

Are there any "catches" to this free offering?

Absolutely! There are three. But they are more than reasonable and I am sure you will agree.

Here they are:

1. Don't sign up <u>unless</u> you are going to fully and completely participate on the webinar. That means you have to do every single exercise that we have you do to help you increase your business. You will have homework to turn in to be sure you are following through.

   Listen-it's not cheap for me to put this process together and just decide to have the tuition fees waived. I am more than happy to do this for people who take this and their business seriously. But anyone who doesn't participate fully will be penalized. That's only fair.

   Ninety percent of people first consider the value of something dependent on how much they pay for it. So, since I am giving you this for free, I need to be sure you do everything to experience that value instead of devaluing this wonderful gift I am giving you for free.

2. There is a $0 USD charge to attend the How To Create An Idea Virus For Your Rapid Authoring And Business Acceleration Webinar (Value $197). However, we will be asking your permission for a "good faith" credit card deposit of $17. That deposit will not be charged to your account unless you miss all or part of the webinar and do not do and turn in your homework.

Honestly, I'm only looking to invest this process in completely committed individuals who are totally serious about feeling the financial benefits of dominating there market place.

3. After you experience the quickly generated income from this webinar, I would like you to send me your testimonial with all the details of how this system has increased your business.

Finally, after you participate in the class and complete the course, you will qualify yourself to participate in something revolutionary in the authoring and publishing field.

Go to the following URL and find out right now and join...

http://AuthorAndGrowRich.com/bonuses/webinar

Again, the reason you are getting this special offer is because you're dedicated to following through by finishing this book. This tells me that you are serious about your business growth and intelligent enough to see opportunity when it's right in front of you.

Ultimately, your authoring and business success will come down to the following two keys (this is what I tell each of my clients before they enter into a business relationship with me):

The Two Keys To Your Authoring And Business Success.

1. You must be willing to challenge your assumptions about success. You must be willing to do what a mentor tells you to do placing your trust fully in the process. Remember, for you to experience quantum leaps in your success it is absolutely necessary for you to work with someone who will reveal to you a tested and proven system. It is necessary to unlock your mind to a whole new way of seeing what is possible for you, your passion, and how to tap into the gold that is literally sitting right underneath you.

2. You must be willing to take focused, out-come driven action. Your success is dependent first on qualitatively seeing the world from a whole new perspective. Then you must be open to working with a mentor who will honestly show you how to achieve the success you have always dreamed of having. This revelation needs to be reinforced by you acting on the specific attitudes and skills that you gain in the context of the market place.

This book is a total waste of your time if you simply glance thru it and fail to use it as a resource guide for your authoring and business venture.

I salute you to taking action on your dream. I commend you to live and leave your legacy as someone who has taken the authoring journey.

To Your Legacy,

GLENN DIETZEL

P.S.

This webinar (value $197) will position you with opportunities that 98% of individuals either don't know of, wouldn't recognize or don't apply in the way that truly allows them to earn the type of money they deserve.

Congratulations on being one of the 2%!

This webinar will showcase to you the power of the possibilities of a lifetime that only come because of your book.

You will also see for yourself how this system has helped thousands and thousands of people globally...ordinary people just like you who wanted to leave and live their legacy today.

Your legacy begins with your book!

Go now and join the rest of your team. It's your time!

http://AuthorAndGrowRich.com/bonuses/webinar

Printed in the United States
105332LV00001B/3/P